Third Edition

Mediation

Third Edition

Mediation

Empowerment in Conflict Management

Kathy Isaacson
The University of New Mexico

Heidi Ricci
The University of New Mexico

Stephen W. Littlejohn

WAVELAND PRESS, INC.
Long Grove, Illinois

For information about this book, contact:
Waveland Press, Inc.
4180 IL Route 83, Suite 101
Long Grove, IL 60047-9580
(847) 634-0081
info@waveland.com
www.waveland.com

10-digit ISBN 1-4786-3993-8
13-digit ISBN 978-1-4786-3993-0

Printed in the United States of America

7 6 5 4 3 2 1

Contents

Preface

Many forces converged into the decision to create this third edition. We appreciate the opportunity to add a third author, Heidi Ricci, who is an accomplished and skilled mediator. She has trained countless mediators and has given us fresh eyes to keep up with the rapidly growing field. It also has been invigorating to see that many of the concepts and foundations that support mediation practice are still alive and strong. We kept many references to those scholars and practitioners who carved the path for mediation. We continue to find their words relevant. Naysayers once told us that mediation is a "trend" and the end of the trend was near. Mediation is no trend. It is a strong force for systems change that gives immense hope to humanity. Finally, we added some timely and relevant exercises and role play scenarios. Many of the role play scenarios came from mediation students who developed them for use in future classes.

We have appreciated the responses and feedback from those who have used this book. Instructors and mediation trainers have indicated that this book often serves as a supplement to a larger focus in training or in a course, such as conflict and communication. It can be used to focus on mediation as a piece of a larger course or could serve as the foundational text of mediation training. We have used this text in mediation trainings followed by internship opportunities in mediation offices in our community. The book also develops a framework for personal use, furthering effective communication in conflictual situations, as much of the feedback we received affirmed the practical and useful nature of the content.

In writing this third edition, we found that study and practice of mediation is still an exciting endeavor. Perhaps it's because beyond the practice, the mediation tools we provide in this book are also life skills that if utilized will not only change your approach to conflict in your professional and personal relationships but change them for the better.

This practical, concise text is guided by a clear set of theoretical principles—an ideal for mediation in our society—and is intended for anyone interested in learning mediation skills. Trainers and teachers appreciate the length, which allows them to provide additional information and insight and to adapt the book to any number of training approaches. Given its readability, it is also appropriate for school and youth mediation programs.

We have maintained the brevity, clarity, and directness of our first two editions. Participants in a training program can read it quickly; they can get an immediate overview of mediation and a summary of necessary skills before practicing as mediators in the classroom or training sessions. We have included some tools developed since the second edition, and we offer an extended appendix of materials for trainers and practitioners.

We want to thank our many students of mediation over the years who have contributed to each new edition of this book.

Introduction

Mediation has become increasingly popular over the last five decades. Because it can be more constructive, comfortable, and cost-effective than traditional adversarial methods, organizations and individuals are using this form of conflict resolution with greater frequency. Mediation affords an opportunity for groups and individuals to work through their differences in an atmosphere in which they can feel safe and which leads to positive outcomes for everyone.

A skilled and impartial third party can help people in conflict understand their conflict as a positive opportunity for change; find common ground; explore creative ideas for solutions; and express their perspectives in ways that can be heard and understood. In this book we present numerous techniques that mediators use to help parties achieve these goals, but mediation is far more than technique.

We think of mediation as an art in which skilled practitioners help individuals and groups achieve positive and mutually agreeable results. Although mediation often ends in a settlement or written agreement, a good mediator aims to achieve much more. Successful mediation involves a number of benchmarks.

The best mediations involve *collaboration at every level*. Participants work together and also with the mediator to create outcomes beneficial to all. In a competition, the objective is to win as much as you can; in collaboration, the objective is to work together so that everyone wins. Collaboration is apparent when the parties stop struggling to prevail and begin a process of joint problem solving.

In mediation, the two parties are not in a contest. The goal is not to find out who is right, who is to blame, or to whom to give credit. The goal is to find the appropriate resolution to the conflict, one that satisfies both parties. Participants can move more easily toward exploring options of mutual benefit if they can safely "let go" of the need to be right or to "win." Thomas Crum (1987) expands on this view in his book *The Magic of Conflict*:

> Conflict Is Not a Contest
>
> Winning and losing are goals for games, not for conflicts.
>
> Learning, growing, and cooperating are goals for resolving conflicts.
>
> Conflict can be seen as a gift of energy, in which neither side loses, and a new dance is created.
>
> Resolving conflict is rarely about who is right. It is about acknowledgment and appreciation of difference. (p. 49)

When mediation is successful, all of the parties learn what is important to them, and each expresses his or her concerns, perspectives, feelings, and ideas clearly and in a way that others can hear and understand. This is the essence of *empowerment*.

Most people feel the need to have at least moderate control of their lives. Gershen Kaufman and Lev Raphael (1983) see this type of power as offering choices for life's decisions. Having choices means the ability to control or to influence conflict situations. Kaufman and Raphael state,

> A sense of inner control is the felt experience of power and having choice over matters which affect us is its wellspring. We must feel able to affect our environment, to feel consulted, to feel we have an impact, to feel heard by those with whom we are in a relationship. To experience choice is to know power. (p. ix)

The mediation process empowers individuals by giving them choices. Most mediation programs require voluntary entry. This entry signals the first choice—to participate or not. Many other choices occur in mediation, including which options to explore, which emotions to show, and the choice to agree on a solution. When power is well managed in mediation, each party is able to become a full, positive contributor. When everyone is satisfied that he or she has done everything possible to achieve the best results, good power management has occurred.

All people have a need to be treated with *dignity and respect*. Mediation affords an opportunity to work through a conflict in a way that builds a sense of personal worth. Because conflict itself can be threatening to one's self-image, mediators give a lot of attention to maintaining respect and protecting disputants from harm. In the best mediations, the disputants themselves work to contribute to a positive atmosphere.

One of the chief advantages of having a neutral third party is that it often helps make the disputants *feel more comfortable*. Just knowing there is a skilled person to guide the process can make the environment feel safe enough for the participants to explore and test ideas, disclose their feelings and interests, and work creatively to achieve constructive results. Many of the techniques presented in this book are designed to help build the kind of environment in which the good work of mediation can proceed.

Mediators continually develop a tool kit that can be used in various situations—the tricks of the trade. But mediators need more than tools. They need good judgment about how to respond and when to use particular techniques. They need to be creative and to think quickly on the spot. And they need to have a strong commitment to a high-quality process.

This process is very important. We want to work in a way that will promote constructive communication, build respect, and lead to positive results. Mediations should be conducted in a manner that is acceptable and workable to the parties themselves. They should feel that the process is designed to work for them. Good process management involves addressing process concerns directly and clearly, being sensitive to the participants' process needs, and encouraging the disputants themselves to be collaborators on process design. As you consider your options in responding as a mediator, ask yourself whether what you are doing helps to build collaboration, respect, and safety.

The following chapters propose an exploration of mediation as a conflict management option that turns conflict into opportunity. Besides the obvious advantages of this process—the savings of time, energy, and money when resolving disputes—there exists a larger view of mediation. The mediation process is a new language, a way of approaching life that can help us discover answers to individual and societal problems. Moving from competitive to cooperative problem solving is a shift of great magnitude, producing opportunities for significant growth and change in today's world.

1

Conflict Management

Student's Journal Entry
The most significant conflicts in my life have always occurred in the same context: interpersonal relationships. Learning to identify all conflicts as having basically the same components helps give me confidence that I have the ability to deal with all of them.

Understanding Conflict

How do you view conflict? When you see or hear the word, is your first response "pain," "trouble," "fighting," or "misery"? If so, you are not alone. The connotation most people have of conflict is a negative one. Studying mediation provides a larger, less polarized perspective, one that contains opportunities for constructive problem solving and a positive attitude toward conflict.

Many conflicts remain negative because individuals do not have the tools to channel differences in a positive direction. The mediation process offers a channel for learning and implementing the communication skills necessary for this movement to occur. In their book, *Managing Interpersonal Conflict*, William A. Donohue and Robert Kolt (1992) explore the potential for constructive conflict. They use the Chinese symbol for "crisis" on the cover of the book. This symbol has two components, one representing "danger" and one representing "opportunity." Conflict can be dangerous when our needs are threatened, and our desires aren't realized—yet an opportunity exists to clarify issues and feelings while taking a step to prevent future conflicts. This chapter explores the dangers and opportunities of conflict and introduces commonly used conflict management strategies, concluding with a brief explanation of options available for disputes.

EXERCISE **"Conflict Connotations"**

As a whole class or in small groups, list the *first* words that come to mind when you hear the word "conflict." Circle the words that have a positive connotation with one color marker and the words with a negative connotation with another color marker.

- Are there more words of one connotation than the other?
- Are there words that fit under both categories? And if so, why is this?
- Continue the discussion by brainstorming for words that lessen the disparity. In and of itself, conflict is not negative; rather it should be considered as an opportunity for change. From an early age, we are taught that being in conflict is negative, probably because words and actions during a conflict can be negative and hurtful. This paradigm shift in viewing conflict as a need for change can help us embrace a new perspective.

Defining Conflict

Although there are numerous definitions of conflict (which is understandable, since human differences exist on a continuum ranging from interpersonal situations to international crises), many of the components of the definition remain constant. Joyce Hocker and William Wilmot (2001) see conflict as:

> an expressed struggle between at least two interdependent parties who perceive incompatible goals, scarce resources, and interference from others in achieving their goals. (p. 41)

Simply put, all conflict starts with unmet expectations.

Consider the following situation in light of the above definitions. Roommates Sue and Jane want to keep the kitchen clean, but Jane wants to do the dishes weekly while Sue wants them done daily. By using the definition above to explore Sue and Jane's conflict, we see opportunities and dangers.

Expressed struggle: Both parties must realize there is a disagreement for there to be a conflict. If Sue had the desire for daily dishwashing but had never made her desire known, Jane would not be aware of the conflict.

Interdependence: Whether we are dealing with countries, companies, families, or friends in a conflict situation, the parties are usually dependent on each other. Their relationship necessitates communication, and their differences produce conflict. If Jane and Sue were not roommates sharing one kitchen, dishwashing duties would not be an issue for them.

Perceived incompatible goals: In a conflict situation, it usually seems that there will be a winner and a loser. Sue and Jane perceive that they cannot each get what they want. Jane sees her plan as incompatible with Sue's and vice versa.

Perceived scarce rewards: Individuals often see their time, energy, money, and other resources as being in limited supply. When there aren't enough of these to go around, conflict can occur. Jane sees no block of time when she could schedule daily dishwashing duties, whereas Sue does not want the daily discomfort of seeing a sink full of dirty dishes.

Interference: Sue sees Jane as interfering with her goal of a clean kitchen; Jane sees Sue as interfering with how she spends her time.

Discussion

1. In the situation with Sue and Jane, we see why the conflict has occurred and what the positions are. What change is needed?
2. Think of some conflict you or someone you know experienced recently: What was the conflict about (expressed

struggle, perceived scarce reward, interference, perceived incompatible goals)? Consider what change was needed. (Example: a couple constantly arguing may need counseling to strengthen their communication skills, or maybe they need to break-up because the relationship is not healthy.)

Words of the Wise

You would think that understanding and handling conflict would be a major priority in our lives. Yet we rarely attempt to understand it. We try to avoid it or resist it. But it always comes back to haunt us. Have you ever avoided keeping adequate financial records only to find yourself paying for it in time and money at tax time? Or have you ever resisted a healthy exercise or nutrition program only to regret it each time you glance at the mirror? How many times have you avoided telling an uncomfortable truth only to find the problem magnified with time, making the eventual telling much more difficult?

—W. A. Donohue and R. Kolt (1992, p. 47)

Donohue and Kolt (1992) add that conflicts can be manifest or latent. Manifest conflict is out in the open and clearly seen or heard. Manifest conflict would be evident if Sue leaves Jane a note saying, “This kitchen is a mess,” and later that day Jane tells Sue, “Who has time to do dishes?” Latent conflict exists when people avoid the issue and do not make their discomfort or displeasure apparent. These latent conflicts are often more intrapersonal (within oneself) as the individual struggles with a situation while avoiding bringing it into the open. The expression of this conflict may be internal but may have external manifestations. For example, a man distressed over a workplace relationship may not share his feelings with anyone, yet his work may be sloppy and his attitude negative.

With a clearer definition of conflict situations, individuals can begin to take steps to promote constructive conflict management. This knowledge can empower individuals when they realize they are taking action to alleviate problems rather than simply hoping a disturbing situation "goes away" or feeling buffeted by events beyond their control.

Conflict isn't always between two people. Think of a decision you have to make, or a conversation you replay over and over in your mind. This is a form of intrapersonal communication, which we can call ***intrapersonal conflict***. Rather than being a struggle between two people, the conflict is a struggle within yourself. Hocker and Wilmot (2018) define intrapersonal conflict as "an internal strain that creates a state ambivalence, conflicting internal dialogue, or lack of resolution in one's thinking and feeling" (p. 3).

Our perceptions drive how we interpret the actions of others and these perceptions can be greatly affected by our intrapersonal thoughts. Imagine you are at a party wearing an outfit your friend convinced you to wear but was totally out of your comfort zone. Throughout the night you notice people looking at you and smiling. If you felt confident in your clothes, you probably would interpret the looks and smiles positively. If you felt uncomfortable, you would probably interpret those smiles and looks negatively. How we read others' nonverbal communication is intrinsically linked to how we feel about ourselves.

EXERCISE **"Conflict Journal"**

Find a partner. Share a conflict situation in which you find yourself or which you read about or observed. Then individually, write about these situations using a two-column format:

Column 1—Describe the event or situation, being as objective as possible. Pretend you are a disinterested third party observing the conflict. What happened or is happening?

Column 2—Record your feelings, thoughts, and ideas concerning the conflict. This includes your own subjective evaluations and judgments concerning the situation. How would you view this conflict from a third-party perspective? Does this viewpoint change how you might have handled the situation? Is this situation fair, just, disconcerting, joyous, curious?

These entries will give you experience separating the objective from the subjective, a useful skill for mediators.

Managing Conflict

Conflict can be constructive or destructive, depending on how we handle it or how we use communication tools. Being aware of this possibility allows us to see a variety of choices in how to manage conflict. Throughout this book, we will discuss tools to encourage effective communication, including: active listening (listening that displays an intent to understand the intended message), reflecting (acknowledging the emotion in a statement or situation), reframing (reconceptualizing a situation to gain shared understanding), attentive nonverbal behavior, and perception checking (whether we see this situation with the same understanding as others). Five strategies—avoidance, accommodation, competition, compromise, and collaboration—are common choices in dealing with conflict situations in daily life. However, before you consider what your conflict strategies are in any given situation (because we often have more than one strategy depending on our comfort level with those involved in the conflict), it's important to understand why we often stay stuck in conflict rather than moving toward resolution. We call this the "train effect".

Focus-Facts-Feelings

What is the driving force on a train? The obvious answer is the engine. The engine has the power to pull a train forward to its destination, while the caboose, at the back of the train, is just along for the ride. The caboose may be valuable for what it carries, but without the engine it would go nowhere. In the train effect, we think of the engine as the facts and the caboose as the feelings. Now think about a conflict. If you watch the news or surf the internet at any given time you will find a plethora of conflicts ranging from politics and the world stage, to your community, to the Kardashians. When in conflict we want to be heard and our feelings acknowledged, but when there are two sides desiring the same thing, there can be lots of shouting and not enough listening. In essence, the train engine now is being driven by feelings (the caboose) rather than the facts and when this happens, the train will eventually stall or derail because the engine is now in the back.

Until "feelings" are acknowledged and people feel heard, they will not be ready to hear the "facts" of the other person's viewpoint. Facts are important. Therefore, when in conflict, it is important the keep the focus on the destination by acknowledging the feelings but sticking to the facts . . . otherwise you will derail the train. People will rarely be open to listening to your facts if you do not acknowledge their feelings (and the same is true for you!). We will be exploring the essential skill of acknowledgement later in the book.

In the following sections, we define each conflict management strategy, examine possible advantages and disadvantages, and explore examples.

Avoidance

Individuals in conflict often decide to avoid the problem area altogether. Unwilling or unable to face the situation, they "vacate" physically, verbally, or nonverbally. This approach can be useful if the conflict is short-lived (someone's sprinkler splashes water on you while jogging by) or minor (waitress refilled your water glass when you said you'd had enough water). For other situations, the drawbacks to avoiding conflict are many: the conflict can escalate; the relationship most likely will not improve; there will still be an issue "stewing" inside the person; and the person passed up a chance to experience a learning opportunity that could be useful for future conflict. An

Student's Journal Entry

I was incredibly offended and mad. The remarks were bad enough but speaking to me like I should understand and agree complicated my feelings and made it personal. I very nearly unleashed a torrent of verbal abuse of my own. Instead, I stayed silent. I didn't know what to do. I felt like I was avoiding in a big way, but I didn't think creating a "scene" with someone I work with in the middle of a busy shift was the thing to do. I have done nothing so far, but it still disturbs me.

example of avoidance occurs when a part-time employee avoids speaking up about an unhealthy working environment. They could avoid physically (quit the job without telling their boss why), verbally (continue answering queries about the working conditions by saying "everything is just fine"), or nonverbally (not say a word and continue to work). The most frequent outcome of avoidance is a perception of a winner and a loser—and a large power imbalance.

Accommodation

A person who puts another person's needs or desires ahead of their own is accommodating that person. Individuals who fail to assert themselves by always giving in seem to be saying that the desires of other people are more important than their own. Sometimes it is too risky to speak up, as in a case where the consequences may be detrimental. Other times if the situation just isn't that important, it may be easier for all involved to put one party's desires first. If a father is interested in watching a news program and his son wants some help on an important project for school the next day, the dad can accommodate by helping with the son's project, knowing he can watch the news later.

Accommodation can be detrimental if one person doesn't value the worth or importance of his or her own needs. If a husband always refuses invitations to attend hockey games despite being an avid fan because he thinks his wife will resent being home alone, he may be being too accommodating. He is also reacting to a *perceived* conflict. If he doesn't discuss the issue, he may have attributed feelings to his wife that do not exist; that is, he may have misread the situation. Accommodating in this situation and many others may result in a win/lose situation.

Competition

Competitive approaches to conflict often involve highly assertive or aggressive individuals who see conflict as a win/ lose situation. One person, usually the more powerful, wins at the other's expense. Competition is a strategy that has its place in clearly defined situations. For example, in a negotiation over the sale of a used car, one party may be bargaining competitively and expects the other party to do the same or risk being perceived as weak or unskilled.

Unless both parties freely define a situation as requiring healthy competition, competitive approaches to conflict can provoke defensiveness in the other party. One person may feel that their needs are threatened and will shift the focus of the conflict away from the original issue to combat perceived threats, attacks, and comparisons. Defending oneself becomes the issue, and there is little chance of resolving the first disagreement. The power struggle that occurs in this situation can change a simple conflict into a multi-issue crisis. Two workers who began discussing the issue of "who gets to use the fax machine first" can find themselves in a battle over "who gets a better salary" and "who treats the customers better."

Words of the Wise

Ultimately, however, conflict lies not in objective reality,
but in people's heads. Truth is simply one more argument—
perhaps a good one, perhaps not—for dealing with the difference.
The difference itself exists because it exists in their thinking.
Fears, even if ill-founded, are real fears and need to be dealt with.
Hopes, even if unrealistic, may cause a war.
Facts, even if established, may do nothing to solve the problem.

—Roger Fisher and William Ury (1991, p. 23)

Compromise

When two parties meet halfway in negotiation, both give up something they want or need and meet somewhere in the middle. Because individuals give up a part of their wants or needs, compromise is sometimes seen as a lose/lose situation. Compromise can be effective in a situation where you have a multifaceted issue and time is short. If two countries are negotiating about a cease-fire and they need an immediate decision, they may each strike three of their requests and agree on one. This approach can also be useful if both parties have tried collaborating (see next section), and the negotiation has fallen apart. If the two countries have worked together for two months with no clear results, they may decide to compromise for the time being until a more appropriate negotiation situation can be arranged.

The disadvantage of this strategy is that both parties often leave the negotiation dissatisfied. It may have been mutually acceptable to end the negotiation this way, but it may not have been mutually acceptable to settle on the compromised terms.

Collaboration

The goal of a collaborative style of conflict management is to produce a win/win situation. Both parties are attempting to satisfy the needs or desires of each side. Collaboration requires a commitment from each side—a desire to work together and to produce a solution that is mutually acceptable. The first hurdle is to reach a mutually agreeable assessment of the issue to be confronted. The next step is often called Issue Framing. It is important to frame an issue in open, non-judgmental questions that invite people to address it together.

Collaboration is most advantageous to people who want to preserve an ongoing relationship—whether spouses, employee–employer, neighbors, or office mates. Collaboration allows parties to experience creative and constructive problem solving, which can be an opportunity to prevent the next conflict. Consider the situation where a landlord wants to raise the rent to pay for building upkeep, but the tenant is unable to pay more. A collaborative negotiation could result in the landlord deciding not to raise the rent as the tenant (a carpenter) agrees to help paint and repair.

Fisher and Ury (1991) outline five important steps in collaborative negotiation. The first step is to *separate the people from the problem*. In the case of the landlord and tenant, the tenant could easily see the landlord as someone who is just money hungry and unfair. Whereas, the landlord might see the tenant as someone who is cheap and doesn't understand the cost of upkeep. These attitudes can quickly spiral out of control as each party sees the other as unreasonable. Once they participate in mediation, both the landlord and the tenant find common ground. The landlord values his property and wants it to look nice; the tenant values having a nice place to live. In understanding their common ground, they can stop seeing each other as the problem and can collaborate on the upkeep of the building.

The second step is to *focus on interests, not positions*. The landlord needed to raise the rent in order to afford the upkeep on the property. The tenant could not afford higher rent. The mutual interest is having an updated building. Again, finding common ground and focusing on that interest allows parties to collaboratively negotiate what they need rather than being stuck in what they want.

The third step is to *invent options for mutual gain*. It's important that each party take an active role in providing ideas to be discussed. The mediator should encourage a variety of ideas and generate "reality check" questions that allow the parties to consider what options will ultimately work best for their situations.

The fourth step is *using objective criteria*. The mediator should insist that the result be based on some objective standard. An example of this would be for the landlord and tenant to agree on the value of the work the tenant would be providing in lieu of the rent. They would research to make sure it is comparable. This step is critical in avoiding future conflict about the rent and the work being provided.

The fifth step is *know your BATNA (Best Alternative To Negotiated Agreement)*. This step emphasizes that no method can guarantee success if all the leverage lies on one side. Consider the case of a divorcing couple selling their home. Rather than simply agreeing to sell, they divert to thinking about all the possibilities if the house is not sold. They need to find the best alternative.

EXERCISE **"Rock, Paper, Scissors"**

Remember the game with this name? Each party mentally chooses rock, paper, or scissors and then when the choice is discovered, there are winners and losers. This exercise is similar in that participants choose *avoidance, accommodation, compromise, competition, or collaboration* (mentally) and then participate in a role play using that conflict management style. This works best in dyads. The following role plays can be used:

1. Two employees, a smoker and a nonsmoker, discuss creation of a new policy regarding smoking at the workplace.
2. A teacher discusses a failing grade with a protesting student.
3. Two parents try to decide on discipline decisions for a son who has been staying out very late at night.
4. Two neighboring countries discuss border control.

Discussion can revolve around issues like:

- How did your style feel to you?
- How did the other person's style affect you?
- Which style was most comfortable/uncomfortable for you?
- Were you ever tempted to switch styles in the midst of a role play? Why?
- How did these styles affect the *power* of the participants?

Use of collaboration may be risky in some cases. For example, a negotiator who initiates with collaboration and then switches to competition risks alienating the other party. Occasionally, a party may seem to be "working with" the other party on a complicated issue. Eventually it becomes evident that the first party was using collaboration as a way to gather enough information and power to "go for the big win."

Collaborative approaches to conflict management are often win/win situations. Parties work to explore options to a resolution that can satisfy both of them. A mutually acceptable, collaborative resolution is usually not a spectacular one for either party, but it is reasonable, workable, and satisfying.

Mediation as a Transformative Process

Conflict management implies an ongoing concern both for the individual conflict situation and the larger situation in which it occurs. Managing this situation supposes that we are not just resolving problems to make room for new problems. Rather, conflict management creates an environment that may effectively diagnose, work through, and perhaps prevent future conflicts.

Robert Baruch Bush and Joseph Folger in *The Promise of Mediation: Responding to Conflict through Empowerment and Recognition* (1994) view conflict management as a means to transform people and situations. These authors contend that as people change during the conflict management process, they develop positive capabilities to deal with differences and challenges. Mediation and other conflict management processes in our society move us toward a "problem-solving" approach—finding solutions and creating specific settlements. The "transformative" approach suggests that if we empower parties to define issues and settlement terms for themselves, they can better understand each other's perspectives and can create more genuine solutions to their problems.

The mediation model presented later in this text follows a transformative approach to conflict management. The goal of the process is not only to have a resolution (in which case the term "conflict resolution" would be more appropriate) but to transform the parties through a mediation process that uses the following definitions of empowerment and recognition:

> *Empowerment*: Strengthened self-awareness
>
> *Recognition*: Expanded willingness to acknowledge and be responsive to other parties' situations and human qualities

A successful mediation means that (1) the parties have been made aware of the opportunities presented during the mediation for both empowerment and recognition; (2) the parties have been helped to clarify goals, options, and resources, and then to make informed, deliberate, and free choices regarding how to proceed at every decision point; and (3) the parties have been helped to give recognition wherever it was their decision to do so (Bush and Folger, 1994, pp. 84–85).

Resolving Disputes

Society has worked out many ways to resolve disputes. Some methods concentrate almost exclusively on settlement. Other forms concentrate more on creating empowerment and constructive relationships. Dispute resolution can be direct, facilitated, or adjudicated, as outlined in table 1.1.

Table 1.1 Basic Types of Dispute Resolution

	Settlement-oriented	Relationship-oriented
Direct	Representative negotiation	Personal negotiation
Facilitated	Settlement facilitation	Mediation
Adjudicated	Arbitration; trial	

Direct Methods

The most common form of conflict resolution is negotiation. Often negotiation is done through representatives. For example, a union steward may negotiate on behalf of an employee; a parent may negotiate on behalf of a child; or a real estate agent may negotiate on behalf of a homebuyer or seller. These are all examples of *representative negotiation.*

Because our society tends to settle serious disputes through the legal system people in conflict are quick to hire an attorney when things go wrong. As a result, representative negotiation is an important part of the practice of law. In fact, the vast majority of lawsuits in the United States are settled through negotiation without ever going to court. Soon after a lawsuit and response have been filed, the attorneys usually attempt to negotiate a settlement, and they are often successful. It is the threat of court, however, that frequently motivates parties to settle in this manner. Since attorneys are charged with the responsibility of representing the best interests of their clients, this kind of negotiation often becomes a power game in which each party hopes that the other side will capitulate to avoid the costs of a court battle.

Of course, we do not always rely on representatives to negotiate for us. Actually, *personal negotiation* is probably the most frequently used form of conflict resolution. Married couples constantly negotiate with one another. Coworkers make decisions about workplace issues. Neighbors negotiate about all sorts of issues. Children are constantly negotiating. We negotiate when we buy a car. In these cases, we rely on our personal skills and relationships rather than those of a representative to see us through the process.

Any time two parties engage in discussion attempting to reach an agreement, they are using personal negotiation. Personal negotiation allows maximum empowerment of the disputing parties, as they have complete control of the situation. At the same time, however, they may or may not negotiate in good faith, and the outcome may or may not be mutually acceptable. Achieving agreement negotiated in good faith is often difficult. Indeed, a dispute may be of such magnitude or so threatening that at least one of the parties will seek the assistance of a lawyer or other representative. Negotiators may also seek the help of an outside facilitator.

Facilitated Methods

For a variety of reasons, the parties to a dispute may seek the assistance of an outside party, often when a stalemate has been reached. Actually, there are many types of third-party intervention. We may seek the help of a mutual friend, counselor, minister, or supervisor. On a more formal level, there are two general worlds of conflict intervention—settlement facilitation and mediation.

Settlement facilitation is a process in which a third party works exclusively to achieve an agreement between the disputants. Although it can be used in a variety of venues such as labor-management relations, settlement facilitation is most commonly seen as part of the legal system. The attorneys themselves can take the initiative to hire a settlement facilitator, or the court may order them to do so. In some cases the court actually appoints the settlement facilitator. Most settlement facilitators are attorneys, judges, or retired judges.

Once an acceptable facilitator is selected, they will meet with the parties. The facilitator typically shuttles back and forth between the parties, helping each weigh alternatives, formulate offers and demands, and craft proposals. The facilitator maintains very strong control of the process, often makes judgments about the respective cases of the two sides, and frequently makes settlement suggestions. This person may also tell the parties what they think will be won or lost in court if a settlement is not reached.

The clear goal of a settlement facilitator is to get an agreement, settle the case, and clear the suit out of the court system. Consequently, there is a great deal of pressure in most settlement facilitations for the parties to agree. Normally, legal considerations dominate the work of settlement facilitation, and facilitators are usually unconcerned with relational issues.

The second general type of intervention is *mediation*. Mediation occurs when a neutral third party facilitates a conversation in which disputants share their stories, discuss their differences, identify areas of agreement, and test options with a possible outcome of a mutually acceptable resolution. Mediators focus on relational issues as well as specific content issues and encourage the parties to create their own solutions within the problem areas. Often two mediators work as a team.

The parties in this process are in control of the information and issues discussed while the mediator keeps an eye on the process. Indeed, mediators are often called "process facilitators" or "process managers" because they suggest flexible rules for the process. At the same time, they work collaboratively with the disputants to establish a process that is acceptable and workable for those involved. In divorce mediation, for example, the parties may deal with division of property and custody settlement, as well as relationship problems that need to be resolved. In a workplace situation, two employees may mediate concerning long-distance telephone calls and communication styles when discussing workplace issues.

Settlement facilitators often refer to themselves as *mediators*, but we see the two processes as sufficiently different to use different terminology. Indeed, in the world of alternative dispute resolution, these two forms have distinct identities.

Settlement facilitators are primarily concerned with only one thing—getting an agreement. Mediators, on the other hand, have broader goals. They usually are more concerned with empowering the parties to collaborate in making appropriate decisions. One decision might be to craft a settlement agreement (although not doing so could be an equally appropriate decision depending on the circumstances). Settlement facilitators work almost entirely in private caucuses (private individual meetings) and discourage direct communication between the parties during the negotiations. Mediators usually prefer to work in a joint session, use caucuses cautiously, and encourage direct communication between the parties. Settlement facilitators generally are not concerned about relationship issues and may even see feelings and relationships as getting in the way, but mediators help parties define an appropriate, constructive relationship. This does not require that the disputants become best friends, only that some modicum of respect and ability to work together, at least during the mediation, is desired. Finally, settlement facilitators are openly judgmental about the disputants' positions and cases, and they often suggest solutions. Mediators, on the other hand, usually try to remain nonjudgmental and empower the parties to develop their own solutions.

Student's Journal Entry

We need to get the message out to the public about what mediation is, as opposed to other dispute resolution processes. I have seen articles in the paper and heard references in other places to mediations "won or lost." This public perception should be considered. Without distinguishing mediation from these kinds of win/lose concepts, will mediation become another legalistic, court-related process?

Adjudicative Methods

Adjudication is a process in which an authority makes a decision between two or more cases based on argumentation. Representatives, usually attorneys, present arguments supporting their respective cases, and the authority decides. The two most common forms of adjudication in our society are arbitration and trial.

Arbitration is a privately arranged process in which an arbitrator (or panel of arbitrators) listens to arguments, reads submitted materials, and makes a determination in favor of one side or the other. Arbitration is usually stipulated in some sort of contract between the parties. The arbitration clause of a contract normally will indicate whether the arbitration is to be binding or nonbinding. Arbitration clauses are found in many real estate contracts, labor-management agreements, and employment contracts.

Trial, of course, is the ultimate settlement forum within the legal system. Depending on the court and the type of case, the decision may be rendered by a judge or a jury. There are several differences between arbitration and trial. Arbitration is usually privately arranged and governed by private contract; trials are part of the public legal system. Arbitrators are private practitioners who may or may not have a law degree and the experience of legal practice; judges are elected or appointed by elected officials and almost always have a legal background. Arbitration usually has less rigid rules of evidence than required in court trials. Finally, arbitration is usually (but not always) faster and less expensive than court.

You probably noticed that the last cell in table 1.1 is empty. There is no widely recognized method of dispute resolution that is adjudicative and also relationally oriented. We are challenged to imagine what such a form would look like. Perhaps the Navajo Peacemaker Court comes close. Here a dispute is brought to the Peacemaker, who is something like a judge. The Peacemaker will listen to the stories of the disputants, but with a special interest in preserving the family, community, and culture of those involved. He will render a decision in the case, but the decision is usually designed to achieve peace, preserve relationships, and honor cultural tradition, with input from the community and the family.

Choosing a Dispute Resolution Strategy

Disputing parties who are interested in selecting a third-party intervention must consider all available options. The following questions can help deal with that choice:

- What goals do we have? Typical goals may be: (1) a quick, easy resolution of the problem, (2) preserving a relationship, (3) preventing problems from escalating.
- What issues do we want to deal with? Content? Relationship? Both?
- How formal of a process do we want to work with? (Do we want to sit comfortably on a sofa with a cup of tea, or do we want to be afforded the formality of a courtroom or conference room?)
- How much power or control do we want over the process or the outcome? (Do we want to speak for ourselves or have someone speak for us?)
- What are the time, energy, and financial considerations?

When parties adhere to the view that conflict is negative, they rush into methods of resolution that enable them to "make it go away" or to "get it over quickly." With a positive view of

Words of the Wise

Well-planned confrontations work out much better than unplanned ones. How much time should you spend planning? Consider the slogan, "There never seems to be enough time to do the job right but always time to do it over." Planning asks that you invest your time on the front end of the problem as opposed to the back end. Waiting until the problem grows large requires significantly more repair work than a little routine maintenance up front.

—W. A. Donohue and R. Kolt (1994, p. 47)

conflict, one that envisions constructive results, individuals can carefully choose a dispute resolution method that suits them and the conflict.

Argument and Dialogue

The methods on the left side of table 1.1—representative negotiation, settlement facilitation, arbitration, and trial—are dominated by argument. Each side presents a case, including positions and claims along with supporting evidence. Influence is usually the clear objective as each side tries to persuade the other directly or through a third party of the validity of its position. Although compromise may be an important ingredient, the initial tendency is to debate the issues.

Words of the Wise

Practitioners tell many stories about their affinity for dialogue. Some expound a grand vision of life as it should be; others refer to a particularly captivating experience that pulls them again and again; and still others tell of having developed an aversion to nondialogic forms of communication and seeking to explore alternatives. Like all virtuosos, there is something both of compulsion and fascination in what we call the grand passions of dialogic virtuosity.

—W. Barnett Pearce and Kimberly Pearce,
"Combining Passions and Abilities:
Toward Dialogic Virtuosity" (1999, pp. 162–163)

The methods on the right side of the table—personal negotiation and mediation—may include a good dose of argument, but another kind of communication is preferred—dialogue. At their best, negotiation and mediation involve a different set of goals. Once the parties realize that they are probably not going to get the other side to give in, they may deal with one another in a new way. Mediators are uniquely suited to help the disputants achieve dialogue.

In general, we can say that dialogue is a process of being clear about one's own perspectives, feelings, and ideas, but it is also about being open to understanding and respecting those of others. As a result, listening is an important part of dialogue. Table 1.2 lists some important differences between argument and dialogue.

The principles of dialogue outlined in table 1.2 are goal ideals for mediation. The spirit of dialogue may or may not be achieved in a particular case, but these principles should always guide our aims in the mediation process.

Table 1.2 Argument and Dialogue

Argument	Dialogue
In an argument, we try to win.	In a dialogue, we try to understand.
In arguments, we compete for speaking time.	In dialogues, listening is as important as speaking.
In arguments, we often speak for others.	In dialogues, we speak mostly for ourselves.
In arguments, we bring up the behavior of others.	In dialogues, we speak from personal experience.
The atmosphere of an argument is often threatening and uncomfortable.	The atmosphere of a dialogue is one of safety.
In arguments, we tend to take sides with others.	In dialogues, we discover differences even among those with whom we agree.
In arguments, we polarize ourselves from those with whom we disagree.	In dialogues, we discover shared concerns between ourselves and others.
In arguments, we feel unswerving commitment to a point of view.	In dialogues, we discover our uncertainties as well as deeply held beliefs.
In arguments, questions are asked to make a point or put the other person down.	In dialogues, questions are asked out of true curiosity and the desire to know more.
In arguments, statements are predictable.	In dialogues, we discover significant new information and insights.
In arguments, our statements tend to be simplistic.	In dialogues, we explore the complexity of the issues being discussed.
Arguments tend to be competitive.	Dialogues tend to be collaborative.

Adapted from the Public Conversations Project

Chapter Summary

Conflict is often about miscommunication, misunderstanding, unmet expectations, a clash of values or goals, or even a power struggle. Whatever the reason for the conflict, viewing it as an opportunity for change can help us to look at the conflict from a new perspective. That change cannot happen, however, until we determine the best way to handle the conflict. As discussed in this chapter, we all have different conflict styles. Knowing your style(s) can help you understand why you react to conflict in the way that you do. It can also help you choose the best way to deal with this conflict (negotiation, mediation, litigation, arbitration or open conversation). Above all, consider what is driving the conflict train. Is it emotions or facts? Seek out what it is that needs to change. And remember, the train will never reach its destination if we don't stick to the facts and acknowledge the feelings!

Key Terms

Accommodation is putting another person's needs or desires ahead of one's own, resulting in a failure to assert oneself. Always giving in indicates that the desires of other people are more important than one's own.

Arbitration (an adjudicative method) is a privately arranged process in which an arbitrator (or panel of arbitrators) listens to arguments, reads submitted materials, and makes a determination in favor of one side or the other.

Avoidance is when individuals in conflict "vacate" physically, verbally, or nonverbally, avoiding the problem altogether.

Collaboration is the goal of a collaborative style of conflict management, which works to produce a win/win situation. It requires a commitment from each side to work together to produce a solution that is mutually acceptable.

Compromise is two parties meeting halfway in negotiation. Both give up something they want or need and meet somewhere in the middle. Because individuals give up a part of their wants or needs, compromise is sometimes seen as a lose/lose situation.

Conflict is an expressed struggle between at least two interdependent parties who perceive incompatible goals, scarce resources, and interference from others in achieving their goals.

Empowerment is enhanced by strengthened self-awareness.

Mediation (facilitated method) is a neutral third party facilitating a conversation in which disputants share their stories, discuss their differences, identify areas of agreement, and test options with a possible outcome of a mutually acceptable resolution.

Negotiation (direct method) is the most common form of conflict resolution, which can be either representative or personal.

Recognition involves willingness to acknowledge and be responsive to other parties' situations and human qualities.

Settlement Facilitation is work by a third party to achieve an agreement between the disputants.

Train Effect in conflict is keeping the focus on the destination by acknowledging the feelings but sticking to the facts . . . otherwise you derail the train.

Transformative Approach empowers parties to define issues and settlement terms for themselves so they better understand each other's perspectives and can create more genuine solutions to their problems.

2

Mediation

An Overview

Mediation has emerged over the last five decades as a preferable means to manage differences in our relationships, families, workplaces, schools, communities, and institutions. When people find themselves in conflict situations, they often decide to "mediate" the issue. Mediation is a method from the field of ADR (alternative dispute resolution) and provides an alternative to adversarial processes and can be an appropriate method to address troublesome issues. "Mediation has been effectively practiced in almost all periods of history, in most cultures and used to resolve a variety of disputes" (Moore, 2014, p. ix). Mediation is a conversation that focuses on the skill of active listening. The basic need of all people regardless of culture is not only to be *heard* but also to *feel* heard! Once we feel heard, we become more receptive to what another person has to say.

Think of the last conflict you had. Were you actually listening to understand the other person's perspective? Or were you busy formulating your argument as they were speaking? Conflict is inevitable in our lives. At first glance, mediation skills may seem simple, but putting the tools into practice can be challenging. As you gain an understanding of a mediator's role and how they guide the conversation, you will be able to manage difficult conversations in your life. Practice will never make you a perfect mediator, but it will make you a better listener and more effective conflict manager!

As a method for bringing interested parties together to work out their differences, mediation provides opportunities for people to find workable solutions that satisfy the interests of all parties. Agreements can be reached sooner and through a less costly process than is true with most other alternatives. Agreements are often more easily implemented in comparison to verdicts and third-party directed decisions.

Most mediation programs are voluntary, and parties choose to come to the mediation table. This aspect of mediation signals to the parties that neither of them alone has the power to bring about the resolution. However, what happens when the mediation is court ordered? As the courts begin to understand the value and cost-effectiveness of mediation, rather than making a decision from the bench, many judges will send parties to mediation first to see if they can work out their differences. Given that mediation is a voluntary process, how can this work? While the parties may be court-ordered to come to mediation, their participation is voluntary. One tool mediators often use to encourage parties to participate is to remind them that rather than having a win/lose situation with a judge making the final decision, mediation is their one opportunity to create an outcome that is mutually agreeable to both sides. This helps parties to adopt a cooperative frame of mind. The lasting implications of this experience of cooperation and the communication skills modeled in the process help parties work together to find a mutually agreeable resolution. In turn, this process may prevent the escalation of conflict.

In a broad sense, mediation encompasses a form of communication that breaks through barriers and builds bridges. The mediator, as a neutral third party, focuses discussions and helps shape the language used, with hopes of reaching a mutually acceptable outcome. This process opens communication channels and creates an atmosphere for problem solving. More specifically, *mediation is a process where parties are encouraged to make clear, deliberate choices while acknowledging the perspective of the other. In this process, a mutually acceptable agreement is one possible outcome.*

Our colleague and fellow mediator, David Levin, uses this definition of mediation: "Mediation is an informed agreement that will stick." The juxtaposition of the words "informed" and "stick" helps parties see they have a responsibility to make decisions for themselves that are workable and reliable.

This book will introduce and explore the stages of the mediation process from the opening introduction, to a storytelling stage, to problem solving, and finally to the resolution or agreement stage. Mediation extends the negotiation process by asking a third party to monitor the process while allowing the original parties to be responsible for their own resolution to the conflict.

Words of the Wise

We have come to believe that mediation's greatest value lies in its potential not only to find solutions to people's problems but also to change people themselves for the better, in the very midst of conflict. Time and again, we have seen people change in small but significant ways through their participation in this process. These changes occur because, through mediation, people find ways to avoid succumbing to conflict's most destructive pressures: to act from weakness rather than strength and to de-humanize rather than acknowledge each other.

—R. A. Baruch Bush and J. P. Folger (1994, p. xv)

Role of the Mediator

The mediator is a facilitator. By guiding the parties through an open exploration of their interests and options, the mediator acts as a manager of the process. In fact, we often call mediators "process managers." And as such, the mediator sets the tone of the mediation from the moment the parties walk through the door. This can start with how the room is set up, to the greeting, to how they guide the parties' discussion.

The mediator is impartial. Unlike a judge or an arbitrator who makes decisions for the party, the mediator remains impartial.

Being impartial does not mean a mediator is without opinions or perceptions. Rather, mediators are alert to biases and prejudices and put them aside so they do not affect or alter the process or the outcome. The mediator does not have a stake in the outcome of the process.

It is helpful to use the metaphor of a recording when conceptualizing impartiality in mediation. If we think of ourselves as constantly in recording mode, we can imagine the vast amounts of information we have stored. Our experiences, teachings, travels, observations, readings, and thoughts are all stored and recalled in certain situations. Think of all of the parties in mediation—each with their own recording of experiences, perceptions, and biases. Mediators, aware of all this divergent stored information, make conscious decisions to *turn off their own recordings* during the mediation process.

Mediators are often deemed "neutral." Neutrality is an attitude and a behavior manifested by the mediator. Most often, the mediator professes no relationship with the parties that could affect the outcome. If there is such a relationship between the mediator and one of the parties, it should be suspended completely during the mediation process. All parties are greeted, seated, addressed, listened to, and responded to in a balanced and nonjudgmental manner.

The mediator offers empowerment. It has been stated often that one of the duties of a mediator is to "balance power" between the parties. A more accurate description is to see the mediator as one who attempts to empower each individual party. "Balancing power" is like comparing mediation to a seesaw. In this view, the mediator acts as the fulcrum, adjusting their position to balance the weight (power) of two unequally weighted individuals. This metaphor implies a judgment on the part of the mediator—deciding which party holds more or less power. For example, a mediator trying to "balance power" in a dispute between an employer and an employee might let the employee speak before the employer, assuming the employer has more power. We disagree with this metaphor. A more accurate description is to see the mediator as one who attempts to empower each individual party, allowing and encouraging them equally to contribute fully to the process and making no assumptions about the power dynamics.

A metaphor for individual empowerment is the community dealing with the emperor in the tale *The Emperor's New Clothes*. No one dares tell the emperor that he is naked (using the conflict management strategy of avoidance). While a judge or arbitrator may reach a verdict of "You're naked," the mediator creates a safe environment and, using communication tools, allows the emperor to save face and realize his condition on his own. This empowering step allows the process to keep moving forward without causing the parties to become defensive or embarrassed. In their book *Communication, Conflict, and the Management of Different,* Stephen Littlejohn and Kathy Domenici (2007) posit that mediation assumes that the parties are competent to manage their own conflicts.

It is important to remember that a mediator does not function as a judge, a counselor, an advocate, or a lawyer. Kolb and Associates (1994) warn that mediator power can be viewed with distrust and some wariness. They note, "by keeping a low profile and getting the parties to do the lion's share of the work, a mediator avoids the risk of becoming another party with an agenda to pursue" (p. 477). Keeping in mind that the ultimate responsibility for resolution rests on the disputants, mediators can remain clear on their roles.

The mediator is a face manager. The mediation process and strategies used by mediators address the need for parties to "save face." "Face" is the image that a person displays in public and most often is used to protect one's greatest vulnerabilities. According to Hocker and Wilmot (2007) "People try and avoid loss of face by defending their self-images against humiliation, embarrassment, exclusion, demeaning communication, or general treatment as unimportant" (p. 87). Mediators can guide parties through a sensitive process with little damage to their images. To do so, mediators must be skilled at identifying possible "minefields" for both parties. By guiding discussions to avoid issues most likely to raise defense mechanisms, the mediator can keep all the available energy focused on the content issue.

The mediator is a role model. Mediators model respectful behavior, promote constructive communication, and set a tone for how the parties can listen to and speak to each other. Mediators are honest with themselves. They communicate in an honest and genuine manner, realizing that they enter into the conflict with the parties and have a responsibility to assist them in creating an environment of collaboration and respect.

Benefits

Mediation is convenient. Sessions can usually be set up in a short time and can be held in a variety of places. Mediations have been held in courtrooms and closets, classrooms and living rooms. Some forward-looking organizations have set up "mediation rooms" with special round tables, comfortable chairs, and anything else needed to ensure a comfortable atmosphere.

Mediation builds durable results. Mediation helps build solutions that are reasonable and lasting. When resolution options are identified by the parties, the mediator encourages focused scrutiny to make sure the solution is workable and realistic for both parties. Mediators question the opinions, suggestions, and solutions offered by the disputing parties to anticipate any problems with the suggested direction.

Mediation is efficient. The mediation process saves time, energy, and finances, especially when compared to adjudication. Little or no time is spent in prior investigation or preparation of documents. Compared to court and attorney's fees, mediation is usually quite affordable. Participants in mediation may pay only a small filing fee ($25–$50) when using volunteer mediators—a common occurrence in small-claims court and community mediation. Private mediators charge as much as $200 an hour, depending on experience, expertise, or program considerations.

Mediation is effective. The effectiveness of mediation can be seen by the often-high rate of adherence to the resolution—and by the improved communication between the parties as a result of participating in the process. When both parties agree to a resolution *they* created, they feel ownership of the agreement—resulting in the willingness and desire to implement the customized and comprehensive agreement. Our work as mediators embraces the concept that "people support what they create."

Mediation is preventive. Another important aspect of mediation is its early intervention in conflict. Attention to issues early in the conflict can de-escalate the problem before it becomes unmanageable. What may seem like a minor dispute—not worth putting time and energy into—may actually offer the best opportunity to avoid irreparable schisms. Recognizing individual conflict handling styles early in the process allows accommodation to be incorporated before the styles become so ingrained that no alternatives are possible. Early intervention, when disputes are more likely confined to a single issue, has a better chance of producing mutually satisfactory, win/win solutions than does a later intervention when the dispute has turned into a full-blown crisis.

Mediation preserves relationships or redefines them in a healthy way. By providing a safe place to display a range of emotions, mediators give parties an opportunity to tap into a variety of feelings. Besides anger, hostility, and rage, parties often explore concern, understanding, and empathy. People are better able to see one another's perspective once they have had a chance to express their own. If an employee and an employer end their working relationship during mediation, they will leave with a better understanding of the situation and the reasons for the termination.

Mediation is private and confidential. Most mediation programs offer a private process where the proceedings are kept confidential. Mediators often tear up the notes they took during the process and promise not to share any of the discussions. Parties often sign a statement assuring that everything said in the mediation room will stay confidential. This promise of confidentiality encourages parties to speak frankly and confidently about issues they might otherwise be hesitant to discuss. There are various perspectives on confidentiality, and we revisit them later in this book.

Types of Mediation

Mediation techniques can be implemented at many points along the conflict resolution continuum. Mediation processes see conflict as an opportunity for learning, growing, and cooperating. These skills and principles can be used in intrapersonal communication (talking to yourself), in interpersonal communication (one-on-one communication), and with schools, families, companies, governments, cities, and countries. Mediation language is beneficial in a multitude of situations where conflict is likely to occur. Whether a student learns mediation skills in a university setting, in a workplace, at a church, in a community, or through participation in a mediation process, these skills are directly transferable to other settings. The following are examples of some uses of mediation today.

Court-connected mediation programs are becoming more prevalent all over the world. In 1998, then President Bill Clinton signed legislation to significantly expand the use of alternative dispute resolution in the federal courts. Metropolitan and district courts often have programs where cases can try mediation before being heard by a judge. In some cases, the judge does look at a case and determines that mediation should be the first step. Attorneys act as mediators in cases where they offer an opportunity to clients to settle the case early. These sessions are often called "settlement facilitation" and use another attorney or a judge as the mediator.

Victim-offender mediation is an option in the juvenile justice system. Convicted offenders meet with their victims to mediate the next step, often restitution. The circumstances of these cases are riveting. One often sees a victim, such as a homeowner who had a car stolen, face an offender, often a teenage child with few opportunities. They both enter the situation full of fear and anger. A typical mediation result in these cases is for the teen to agree to some type of community service or to work for the homeowner to repay the damages.

Family mediation covers a number of situations. Divorce mediation deals with concerns over property, custody, finances, etc. while attempting to build a relationship that will continue as the couple raises the children. Parent-child mediation often lasts two or three sessions and discusses issues like curfews, money, cars, and respect. Entire families can mediate around similar issues or can make a number of decisions with the help of a mediator.

Church mediation can heal divisive church conflicts, attend to denominational problems, or help individuals manage difficult issues.

School conflict management programs are thriving in communities around the world. These are usually peer mediation programs where children are trained as mediators to help their peers address conflicts that may occur. Whether on the playground, in the lunchroom, or in the classroom, the children learn valuable methods and skills for problem solving and communication. Special education programs also offer mediation to families who are dealing with issues for their gifted and challenged students.

Workplace mediation is also a blossoming field in employment situations. Some mediation programs are internal, where employees are trained to mediate for other coworkers. The city of Albuquerque has a model peer mediation program for employees. Other programs are external, such as the Equal Employment Opportunity Commission, which offers mediation services in cases of discrimination, sexual harassment, and other civil rights issues. One of the finest external programs is the EEOC mediation program of the U.S. Postal Service, in which experienced and trained mediation contractors meet with employees and management to help resolve their disputes.

Land use issues can be brought to mediation. Mediators often facilitate issues between the developer, neighborhood, and city for land use issues. Neighborhoods and communities can mediate concerning situations that may cause them conflict.

Environmental problems can be addressed by mediation at many junctures in the process. Sometimes the issue is brought to the foreground by mediation very early, such as when pollution is just beginning. In other instances, mediation occurs when the problem is full-blown, such as when a forest has been dangerously depleted, or a bird is nearing extinction. Environmental cases are often complex and lengthy, bringing multiple stakeholders to the table.

International disputes are often brought to mediation. Boundary issues, cease-fires, and civil problems can use high-profile international mediators like former President Jimmy Carter. Carter has mediated all over the world, helping countries and their leaders communicate in a new way.

Online Dispute Resolution (ODR)

In this age of social media, communication online is a medium that cannot be overlooked. Online Dispute Resolution uses technology to manage conflicts among people. ODR is a process for addressing issues for those who previously did not have access to a platform for managing conflict. Despite its popularity, there are various perspectives for ODR's benefits and legitimacy. Katsh (2007) describes it like this:

> While courts and legislatures have been struggling to design legal rules that have authority in cyberspace, there have been a range of successful efforts in Online Dispute Resolution (ODR). Online dispute resolution uses the communication of information and the processing of information to negotiate, mediate and arbitrate online. These systems are important not only for resolving conflicts but for fostering environments in which agreed upon rules and standards can emerge. (p. 97)

ODR can encompass a variety of online mediums, including mediation via phone, email, text, and online forums. In our state-mandated mediations, these online or phone mediations have been an important tool—particularly if a parent is incarcerated and can only participate by phone, or an attorney is on the road. Most recently, we had a mediation that encompassed participants (parents, attorneys, and social workers) in three different counties. Some participated by phone, and others used an online forum. ODR can be challenging because the mediator is missing the valuable input of nonverbal communication. In addition, there can be noise distractions or technical difficulties.

While it might seem strange to hold mediation via email, it gives people time to do their research before responding. If the conversation becomes heated, there is time to cool off before responding. The downside is in misconstruing the meaning behind the message, since we are unable to see or hear the nonverbal communication of the participants. ODR, like all other types of alternative dispute resolution, has drawbacks and benefits. In this age of fast-growing technological advances, online dispute resolution will continue to grow in popularity as a convenient form of managing conflict.

Companies such as eBay and PayPal use ODR as do many courts and government organizations committed to increased access to justice. Do a quick web search for videos explaining ODR and you will see a variety of uses.

EXERCISE

Privately, write down some answers to these questions:

1. Can you remember a conflict that arose online? How did it occur? What was the result?
2. Can you think of a personal conflict you were involved in that may have been better resolved using technology and online methods? How might you have set up that process?

In small groups, share your responses to these questions and discuss how use of ODR may assist with personal conflicts in college students.

When Mediation Is Effective

If parties are to mediate successfully, they need some degree of communication competence. They need minimal communication skills and the ability to follow the structure provided by the mediation process. Parties also need to have some desire to work through the problem. Since participation is voluntary, mediators work with people who have agreed to "come to the table," often seen as the first agreement in the process.

There are other conditions that make settlement in mediation more easily achievable. Successful mediation can occur without these conditions, but cases that include these components will more likely satisfy the parties:

- a previous history of cooperation
- no long history of dispute, distrust, or litigation
- a workable number of issues in the dispute
- moderate or low hostility toward each other
- external pressure to settle (for example, one party faces a time constraint)
- limited psychological attachment to each other
- adequate resources that can be divided

Mediation also can be effective if all of the parties involved are conscious of the goals. Most parties will have a goal of resolution. However, this "resolution" may be very broad. To some, it may mean simply being heard, to others it may mean job security, while to others it may mean getting a good night's sleep. The goal of the process is to support the negotiation between the disputants as they move toward resolution. The goal of the mediator is to set guidelines that provide safety and balance for the parties involved and to assist each party in understanding him- or herself and the other party. One of the most important jobs of the mediator is to identify the differing goals that must flow together before a solution can be reached.

Student's Journal Entry

Doing role plays without settlement objectives made my curiosity and interest in the participants' stories much more genuine and appeared to help the participants relax.

Remembering that conflict is normal and inevitable, mediators can help individuals work through their disputes while offering behaviors and language to be mirrored and utilized in any relationship. The mediation model can be a powerful tool for healing the anxiety that often accompanies conflict and implementing fair solutions. Success is attained when a mediator uses effective communication techniques to facilitate a process where individuals become more cooperative negotiators.

EXERCISE ***"Dismantle the Definition"***

Using the following definition of mediation, experiment with removing components and note what kind of process results.

Mediation: A confidential, voluntary process where a neutral third party facilitates negotiation between two or more parties with mutually acceptable agreement as one possible outcome.

Remove one word or phrase from the definition. How does this change the definition?

Does this change make the process similar to any of the other dispute resolution processes?

How would this change affect the participants? The mediators? Society?

Chapter Summary

Mediation is a cost-effective dispute resolution process that can be used in a variety of situations to help parties work through their conflict. It is the mediator's job to bring balance, neutrality, and a safe space for parties to be heard and to explore possibilities of a mutually agreeable resolution. Keep in mind, one does not have to become a professional mediator to reap the benefit of using basic mediation tools in everyday life. Conflict is inevitable in our lives, how we deal with it can make all the difference in creating the outcome we desire.

Discussion

1. The mediator is a facilitator. By guiding the parties through an open exploration of their interests and options, the mediator acts as a manager of the process. In fact, we often call mediators "process managers." Discuss ways in which a mediator might manage "the process."

2. Being impartial does not mean a mediator is without opinions or perceptions. Rather, mediators are alert to biases and prejudices and put them aside so they do not affect or alter the process or the outcome. Brainstorm some ways a mediator can remain neutral, even if they think one party is right and one is wrong.
3. Mediators model respectful behavior, promote constructive communication, and set a tone for how the parties can listen to and speak to each other. Name some specific ways in which a mediator can model positive behavior.

Key Terms

Alternative Dispute Resolution (ADR) provides an alternative to adversarial processes and can be an appropriate method to address troublesome issues.

Mediator is a neutral third party who encourages participants to make clear and deliberate choices while acknowledging the perspective of the other. In this process, the participants explore a mutually acceptable agreement as one possible outcome.

Online Dispute Resolution (ODR) is a dispute resolution process where the mediator and the parties use technology to negotiate or mediate conflicting issues.

3

A Mediation System

Mediation is best when it is a proactive process. Especially if used early in a conflict, it can prevent further escalation, teach participants new communication skills and methods to address their differences, and can encourage personal responsibility in decision making. Mediators feel hopeful when they realize that participants in their mediation have a recently formed (or discovered) conflict and want to address it immediately. These participants are often apologetic, wondering if their "problem" is big enough to bring to mediation. Experienced mediators know the benefits of this early intervention. How about you?

If you like to avoid or ignore conflict (and there are many of us out there!), you may be hesitant to consider addressing difficult issues. As you better grasp the mediation system and practice the skills we discuss in this chapter, you will see a marked difference in how conflict can make changes for the better in your everyday life. The only way a mediator becomes experienced is through learning the tools of the trade and using them in both their personal and professional lives.

When organizations or individuals are concerned about their working or living environment and want to establish a place where people can prevent or manage their differences in everyday life, they often develop environments that incorporate many of the same characteristics as that of a mediation process.

After years of working with organizations, communities, leaders, and especially workplace teams, we have found five characteristics of "mediation systems" that are proactive and preventive. These characteristics overlap and occur in conjunction with each other.

Characteristics of Constructive Mediation

We offer five characteristics of constructive mediation as a basis for encouraging seamless conflict management within and among individuals in their daily lives and work routines: collaborative communication, power management, process management, safe environment, and face management.

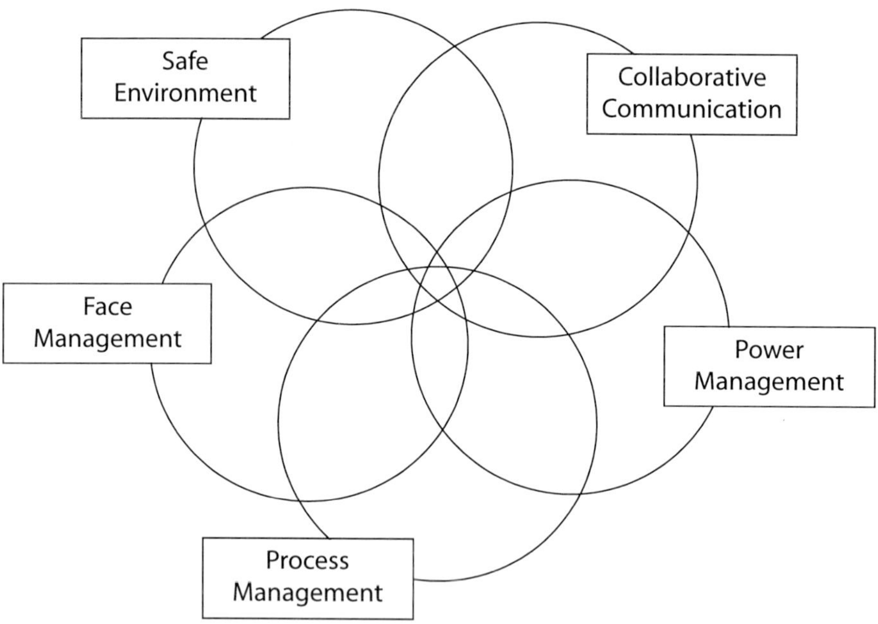

Figure 3.1 The Characteristics of Constructive Mediation

Collaborative Communication

Collaboration is much more than merely "working together." As discussed in chapter 1, we know that when people collaborate, they are working together as well as striving to reach shared goals and achieve their own interests. When collaboration is used as a preferred method of problem solving, it is often seen as "win-win." In their book *Getting to Yes*, Fisher and Ury (1991) encourage people who are negotiating over conflicting interests to focus on the problem, not the people. If you visualize a collaborative process, you see two people sitting on the same side of the table, intently examining the "problem" in the middle of the table. Here, there is the possibility that both sides can walk away from the situation satisfied with the results, having worked together to build a mutually satisfactory solution. With the opposite scenario, people are separated by the table. They are angrily silent or engage in personal attacks rather than reviewing the problem.

When collaborative communication is being used, both sides will be attempting to satisfy their own interests *and* those of the other party. This requires a commitment from both parties. More time and energy is usually needed for collaboration than in typical adversarial problem-solving processes. This time and energy is well spent, as collaboration can be preventive, encouraging parties to work through a set of issues.

The collaborative discovery process often resolves other potential issues before they create road blocks. Collaborative communication offers opportunities for creativity and constructive problem solving. Collaboration has the best chance of occurring when another of the five characteristics, process management, is in place. Adopting a collaborative attitude while considering and constructing an environment that allows careful consideration of mutual goals is an important step toward constructive mediation.

The objective is collaboration, but the question is how does the mediator help parties buy into the concept that collaboration will get them where they need to be? As Gray (2004) notes, collaboration to find an agreeable solution becomes exceedingly difficult because stakeholders have vastly different ideas about each other that affects how they frame issues and the interaction process. The mediator's role is to help parties change harmful perceptions.

We often mediate for the Department of Children, Youth, and Families. This is a very unique type of mediation because we deal with abuse and neglect cases with multiple parties around the table: parents, social workers, attorneys for the parents, the attorney for the state, and the attorney for the children. By nature, this can be a very contentious meeting. At the beginning of the case there is often much confusion and many people have not met one another before. The mediation can be highly charged and emotional.

As mediators in cases like these, we first express our appreciation for everyone being at the table. In our introduction, we acknowledge the fact that this can be a stressful and confusing time but that it is also an opportunity for everyone to be together—outside of a courtroom and without the judge—to understand what is going on, what the needs of the family are, and to get to the same page. Using this opening affirms that we are there to work together in the best interests of the children, which can change mentalities from "us against them" to "we." The opening plants the seed of collaboration. A good mediator will continue to point out *common ground* throughout the mediation to reinforce this ideal.

Here is a simple example of this type of case. The state (social workers) says that parents are not showing up for their mandatory counseling or meetings. The mediator would not ask, "Why aren't you showing up?" Instead, the question would be framed as, "What is preventing you from going to your counseling session?" More often than not, the parents' response is, "We wanted to go but didn't have a ride or our ride cancelled at the last minute." As mediators we would then ask the social worker if there is anything that could be done to help the parents. Brainstorming could result in the state providing a bus pass or recommending a program called *safe ride,* which is available to bring people to various appointments.

By using a difficult issue as an invitation to collaboration, mediators guide the process from *us vs. them* to *we are now collaborating*. They explore how parents can work toward the goal of having custody of their children returned to them. It also creates a situation for the parties to see one another as people and not just as the problem.

EXERCISE "Seeing People as People and Not the Problem"

https://snapjudgment.org/silver-dollar-lounge

This twenty-minute NPR program examines the move toward collaboration. Afterwards, as whole class or in small groups discuss the impact occurring when Daryl Davis chose to put this concept into action. How might adopting this paradigm shift make a difference in your future conflicts?

Student's Journal Entry

Through listening to the stories of both disputants, several shared interests can become immediately evident. These shared interests smooth the transition from conflict to agreement. They are important steps in the collaboration process.

When people utilize collaboration, they experience a greater chance to preserve ongoing relationships. These relationships may be "working" relationships, not necessarily friendships. Collaborative communication can be used for very pragmatic and efficient working relationships, as well as intimate and deeper social relationships. *What does collaborative communication look like?*

In a collaborative environment:

- Participants have shared goals or priorities.
- Participants rely on each other for achievement of these goals or priorities.

- Participants assert their own position without demeaning the position of the other.
- Participants commit to processes in which all the appropriate people participate.
- Participants show concern for work goals as well as relational goals.

Power Management

We know that in any situation where differences arise and conflict occurs, power dynamics are a concern. In win-lose situations, the parties with the most power usually win! Power can be expressed as money, time, energy, communication competence, status, or any other scarce resource. Managing this power helps all the participants contribute, empowering them to participate fully in the process. Discussions of mediation and other forms of dispute resolution often revolve around the use, misuse, and manipulation of power. When a situation exists with both conflict *and* an imbalance of power, managing the situation effectively requires skillful power management.

Donohue and Kolt (1992) believe that to understand power one needs to understand how people manipulate dependencies. According to the principle of least interest, the person with the least interest or investment in a relationship has the most power because that person has less at risk. If so inclined, they can take advantage of the fact that the other party has more to lose. In a conflict situation, the least empowered party depends on the powerful party for many decisions and opportunities. For example, in a conflict between a boss and a subordinate, the subordinate depends on the boss for the job, wages, advancement, and self-esteem. Power is a relational concept.

> Power really comes down to a dependency issue. The more people try to control one another, the more they confirm their interdependency. A couple that is very much in love controls each other's lives. People that love their leaders depend on those leaders for guidance. Love and dependency give those leaders tremendous control over their followers. (p. 91)

Another variable used when analyzing power is the pattern of accommodation in the relationship. Roxanne Lulofs (1994) encourages exploration of who is the more accommodating in the relationship and what the possibilities are for change, noting particularly which person labels the conflict.

> Generally, people with less power accommodate more and are asked to change more radically than those with more power. Powerful people accommodate less, have the opportunity to label the conflict or define its parameters, and have the least interest in ensuring that the resolution of the conflict meets the needs of all the parties involved. (p. 158)

The mediation process is a nonjudgmental forum where relational dependencies can be minimized. As mediators treat each of the parties with dignity and respect, an example is set for how parties can listen to and treat each other—in other words, a model for interaction is established. The message is conveyed that the parties are viewed equally. If one party seems to be accommodating or "caving in," a mediator can gently probe the consequences and implications of the "submission," making sure the decision is a responsible and realistic one.

Student's Journal Entry

There's so little that I've been good at in life, that when I found out I was good at fighting, I pursued it with a vengeance. Mediation has given me an opportunity to see how others try to win in a healthy way. It's given me a chance to teach people a way of resolving things without beating the hell out of each other.

Process Management

We once watched a colleague, Scott Hughes (ADR professor at the University of New Mexico Law School), make some salsa while discussing mediation. We equated each of the ingredients of the salsa with an "ingredient" of mediation. In mediation you will encounter some spicy hot peppers, some tangy lime juice, and some tasty herbs. The main ingredient, the tomatoes, represented the "process" in mediation. Process management involves attention to the "how" of a conflict management environment, as well as the "what." In situations where participants are addressing the "how," they are discussing methods for communicating, making decisions, exploring differences, deliberating options, and agreeing on next steps. The mediation process begins the moment people walk through the door and doesn't end until everyone leaves. The mediation process is two-fold. One part guides the structure of how a mediation is conducted (which we will take a closer look at in chapter 4). The second part is the flow of the mediation, which involves understanding the needs and positions of each party and determining how to approach the discussion.

Words of the Wise

One of the first ways of innovating is to seek clarification of the rules at the table. If they don't fit, you can negotiate to change them. . . . These kinds of rule changes are essentially innovations that make it possible to create a process where the other ways of being can become manifest and effective. They serve to interrupt the assumption that the process will be business as usual—a tedious struggle for dominance power.

—Phyllis Beck Kritek,
Negotiating at an Uneven Table (1994, pp. 267–268)

When a problem arises, people who utilize good process management will resist the temptation to jump right into the content of the disputed issue. They will take some time to ask, "How should we address this issue?" Sometimes the ensuing conversation is lengthy, such as a decision to create an eight-hour retreat to explore the issue. Other times, the process is a quick one, as in situations where the group says, "Let's complete this task now and bring up the other aspects at our next staff meeting."

Once when teaching a conflict and communication class, we offered the students an opportunity to collaborate on the creation of a final exam. The first question asked of the students was "How do you want to create the exam?" not "What should be on the exam?" The students spent two hours discussing a method of creating the final exam, and rich learning about process management occurred.

When effective process management happens, you will hear questions and statements such as:

- How should we have the discussion?
- Who needs to be involved?
- Where and when should we address this issue?
- How much time should we set aside for the meeting?
- Do we need someone to direct the process? A facilitator?
- How should we create an agenda? Do we have goals or objectives?
- What communication guidelines or ground rules do we need?
- What resources do we need? A flip chart? Lunch? Other reports, books, or information?

The answers to questions such as these give people a trustworthy map to follow as they address the difficult issues that face them. With a clear process to follow, participants can be free to attend to the issues at hand.

EXERCISE **"Process Management in Our City Meetings"**

In groups of five, decide on a *meeting process* and/or *guidelines for communication* so you can have a productive meeting. You are five city managers of different departments for the City of Anytown. You have weekly staff meetings and encounter conflict because of differing opinions. Discuss how you can hold these meetings effectively so you can make productive decisions and move forward with your work. Share your results with the class.

Safe Environment

Recently we were mediating a dispute and one of the parties asked for a private meeting (caucus) before the session began. This person shared that he did not feel safe and did not want to take part in the mediation. He was intimidated by the other party and by some facts about the case that made him fearful. We immediately shared this fact with the other party; after some discussion, everyone made a decision that the session would not continue. Mediation requires an environment where parties feel safe. They need to explore their differences productively and without threat. Of course, the above case could have gone in many different directions. The parties and the mediators could have discussed some options to make the process safe for everyone. We have worked in situations where the parties promise not to bring up certain subjects or to call each other certain names. In one mediation, we agreed to a ground rule that we would only talk of the future and what could be done to move forward. That session avoided discussion of any events in the past.

Pre-mediation is a valuable tool for mediators in preparing their approach to a mediation. In the pre-mediation process, the mediator contacts the parties to gain an understanding of each party's perspective on the issues they wish to discuss in the mediation. For the mediator, it is a time to discover concerns and to build an early rapport and trust. One downside mediators need to be mindful of is not to formulate preconceived biases. Pre-mediation is not mandatory for a mediation to have a positive outcome, but it can be beneficial. It can occur on the phone, in a separate meeting, or at the mediation space before the proceedings begin.

We have learned much about safe environments from our colleague Murray Anderson-Wallace. He encourages organizations (and the individuals in them) to show their differences openly. In those situations, groups who are working together can find pathways for productive action. They see the positions and perspectives of their fellow collaborators and can be comfortable offering their own positions and perspectives. Without such free expression, participants can feel unsafe or uncomfortable. In those situations, they may withdraw or refuse to contribute. They may lash out in unproductive ways and perhaps even quit the job or the relationship. Mediators act as facilitators; they are not looking to place blame, find fault, or punish or reward individuals. This lack of "evaluation" gives participants a chance to feel safe enough to air concerns.

In mediation, we often discuss communication guidelines that help create a comfortable and safe environment. When parties agree to "uninterrupted speaking time," they are indicating that respectful listening will be occurring. When constructive process management is evident, participants can trust the process to take them to all the issues they need to address at that time, further enhancing the safe environment. Finally, when people feel they can contribute without threat of personal attack or embarrassment, they can be creative in their problem solving, generating options for resolution that may not have come up otherwise.

While it is preferable for all parties to meet for a mediation, there may be concerns about physical and emotional safety that do not make gathering together the best way to proceed. One example would be in a situation of a divorce where the parties have domestic violence issues and possible restraining orders. Given that the court expects the parties to decide parenting plans and division of the marital assets and debts, the mediator may choose to *bifurcate* the mediation. This means the parties remain in separate rooms, and the mediator goes back and forth between them negotiating the terms of the divorce. This approach can be beneficial to the victim of domestic abuse in helping them to participate while feeling safe doing so.

The following guidelines for communication were created in a retreat with the executive management team of a large multinational company. They built these as an example of effective process management, collaborative communication, and commitment to a safe environment.

1. Our management team can depend on each other to fulfill commitments to each other.

2. Our management team is comfortable delegating decision making to others where appropriate.
3. Our management team meets its obligations to each other.
4. Our management team acts in a timely manner and sticks to its schedule.
5. Our management team collaborates to make choices that satisfy all appropriate parties.

Face Management

In Japan, there are words to describe the often-incompatible presentation we make of our public versus private selves. *Tatemae* is the "outside face" one presents publicly; *honne* is the "inner face," which is one's private—and often more honest—thoughts.

Individuals in a conflict management situation deal with a variety of "face" issues. People often have an image of themselves that they wish to maintain in their interactions. When confronted with a conflict situation, a person's identity, or face, can become vulnerable or threatened. If face issues are not dealt with, the conflict stagnates there, and the original issues are never addressed. For example, in a divorce and child custody mediation, the couple could find themselves discussing or arguing about "who is the better parent" instead of which parent will have the children for Christmas. To understand the different aspects of face issues, it is helpful to look at types of face needs and how mediators can deal with face issues.

S. R. Wilson and Linda Putnam (1990) discuss four different kinds of face needs that motivate people to pursue their goals. Individuals can maintain, save, attack, or support face. When trying to preserve one's image as a respected, competent, and trustworthy person, one is *maintaining* face. A car salesperson can maintain face by stating the number of happy customers they have. A therapist can give a long presentation about their dedication to preserving the confidentiality of clients. A teenage boy can tell stories of how he was the first to finish building a table in shop class. By bolstering positive personal attributes, individuals can maintain face and protect themselves from possible attack in those areas.

Littlejohn and Domenici (2007) describe facework as follows. Autonomy face is a sense of independence and choice. A teenager expresses autonomy face as they try to convince their parents they are mature enough find their first job or ready to drive to the store on their own for the first time. Fellowship face is a feeling of wanting to be included and accepted. Many college students join fraternities or sororities to have that sense of belonging with their "brothers" and "sisters." People they know will support them. Competent face is the perception that you know what you are doing, that you are effective and can make a mark. This is the face we would show when we are applying for a job.

It can become necessary to *save* face when it has been damaged or attacked. Regardless if the "attacks" are real or imagined, people need to repair the damaged image in some way. One can save face by shifting attention away from the attack, changing the subject, minimizing the issue, or joking about it. Face saving is also accomplished by denying the attack or rejecting it ("I didn't inhale" "I have never lied on my income tax"). Persons can save face by putting themselves in a more defensible position by changing their story or making the issue more vague ("What I really meant to say is . . ." "Whether that is true or not, this is the most important point"). These are defensive moves that enable people to repair an image they are concerned with keeping.

People can also attempt to deal with face-saving needs by *attacking* the other's face. By making the other person seem distrustful or unworthy of respect, individuals feel they are portraying themselves as more respectful or trustworthy. This tactic is most evident in advertising campaigns where companies attack the credibility of the competitor's product to make theirs look better. In the world of politics, attacks on the opposing candidate are an effort to bolster the face of the attacker. Such situations can easily get out of control and lose focus on actual issues.

Meeting the face needs of the other to accomplish the goals at hand shows *support*. Face-supporting tactics often reduce the other's need to attack, even if the two parties still disagree on the issues at hand. In a divorce mediation, a parent can support the other's face by noting, "You are great with the children" or "You have consistently shown up on time for our meetings."

In 2000 when the grandmothers of Elian Gonzales (a young boy from Cuba rescued from a sinking boat in Florida), arrived in the United States to negotiate for his return, a visit was arranged between them and the boy in a safe, private place. When they returned to Cuba without the boy, at least they were able to reclaim some dignity and purpose for their visit. Face-supporting skills can be used by mediators or by individuals in negotiation to ensure a smoother and more successful process.

When face issues are not addressed in conflict situations, destructive cycles can occur. For example, discussions digress to escalating face attacks or competing attempts at face maintenance. These cycles can impede attempts to manage conflict. Talk about face issues changes the focus away from the real issues. One party might "cave in" if he or she is unsuccessful at saving face. Third-party interventions can break such cycles by reducing the threat to face and modeling a more flexible and creative process that avoids the disruptive competitiveness. As a protector of face, a mediator closely watches the nonverbal and verbal communication of all participants to ensure everyone's safety and comfort level as they participate. This close scrutiny of facework also tells the mediator when it may be time to reframe a comment or acknowledge emotions.

Mediators have the tools to allow disputants to maintain face. Mediators using active listening techniques can reframe an issue by translating inflammatory remarks into neutral language. They can redirect attention to the issue by removing words that have the potential to attack face from the restatement of the problem. The comment "She's such a liar; how can I believe that the check will arrive on time?" can be reframed by the mediator as "So you are concerned with receiving your payment on time." This reframed statement takes out the face attack ("liar") and puts the focus on the issue. If the issue is an interpersonal one concerning a habitual liar, the statement can still be reframed neutrally: "I hear that you are feeling upset by her dishonesty." By reflecting feelings, the mediator takes the emphasis off of the "liar" and onto the "feeler."

EXERCISE **"Face Examples"**

Find examples of autonomy, competent, and fellowship face in the following video clips on YouTube. Keep in mind, there may be more than one example of each face in each video.

1. This first video is from the film *The Lord of the Rings: The Fellowship of the Ring*. The council is discussing who should return the ring to Mordor.
   https://youtu.be/TrJJ6ncp1fc; *LOTR: The Fellowship of the Ring*, Extended Edition, "The Council of Elrond Part 2"
2. The second clip comes from the movie *Erin Brockovich*. A large law firm has been recruited to help with her lawsuit.
   https://youtu.be/AZMg4vFcRQs; "Two Wrong Feet in Ugly Shoes," *Erin Brockovich* (7/10) Movie CLIP (2000) HD

EXERCISE **"Face-Needs Identification"**

In the lines below, find the face needs. Identify whether the employer and/or the employee are maintaining, saving, attacking, or supporting.

Employer:

1. I spend almost all of my time supervising you people!
2. The report will not be ready on time because I had more important things to do.
3. I am happy to have an employee like you who arrives at these meetings on time.
4. Did you notice that I completed the last three reports on time?
5. If only we had competent secretaries like the people in the office down the hall.

Employee:

1. It is miserable working with a dictator like you.
2. I spend all my time trying to decipher your writing.
3. Of course I didn't type up the memo; I thought that was Mary's job.
4. I have arrived at every staff meeting on time.
5. It is so encouraging to us employees when you provide these donuts and coffee.
6. I have never made a mistake on a budget projection yet!

Face management occurs when people acknowledge and validate the disputants. Expressing positive statements maintains face and sometimes saves face by avoiding face attacks. Participants can commend the others on an area of agreement instead of despairing over the three areas of impasse. By noting even small successes, participants can feel responsible for the accomplishments and be more likely to examine their roles in the dispute. Mediators can support face with statements such as: "This certainly is a highly emotional conflict, and I am pleased at the common interests you've discovered and the one area of agreement. Congratulations!" or "You are each making a great effort to understand each other. John, it seems difficult for you to accept Mary's lifestyle, but you seem to be attempting to see her point of view. Mary, I noticed your distress at the possibility of moving, but you are collaborating with John toward solutions in a positive way." All participants can note the image others are seeking to maintain and offer statements to support that image.

A mediator is a "face manager" for the parties in conflict. When mediators encourage parties to separate the people from the problem, the focus is taken off of the potentially "failed" relationship. Whether husband-wife, teacher-student, employer-employee, salesperson-customer, or neighbor-neighbor, the relationship may be entangled by feelings such as jealousy, anger, betrayal, or hurt. By dealing with relationship issues separately and then viewing a shared problem that the disputants can resolve together, all parties can begin to see their commonalities. Leslie Fagre (1995) notes,

> From the beginning of the session, mediators stress group efforts and shared goals of the process. At different times throughout the session, mediators may commend the disputants for their hard work and cooperative spirit and remind them of the progress they have made together. (p. 3)

Mediator strategies and process goals can be a valuable aid to parties in conflict. By minimizing differences and encouraging a search for commonalities, parties can move forward without fear of losing face. Substantive conflict can be productive. It stimulates thought about a specific problem, and both parties' opinions can be pooled to create a good solution. Affective conflict, such as face issues, creates an unsettling atmosphere that frustrates those involved and diverts their attention from the real issue. They are much more likely to engage in avoidance or escalation behaviors than in cooperative decision making.

By approving and supporting flexibility, the mediator can model what Lulofs (1994) calls *conflict competence*. She notes that

> threatening another person's self-image in a conflict puts the focus on restoring the image rather than on dealing with the issue in the conflict. Threats to face are created largely when people lock themselves and others into untenable positions because they equate flexibility with inconsistency. (p. 193)

In a face-managing system, people can accept the parties' right to change their minds. Compromise later in a negotiation or discarding a bottom line can be seen as "selling out" to some participants. As mentioned earlier, this "selling out" or "caving in" can alert people to a need for more reality checking, but it can be acknowledged in a way that saves face. By remarking neutrally about a new position or interest and noting the difference from an earlier stated interest, people signal a flexible process that can include changing one's mind and, thus, creating face maintenance.

EXERCISE **"Five Characteristics"**

In this chapter, we've discussed the five characteristics of a constructive mediation. Divide into small groups and discuss conflicts you've had. Share positive or negative examples of the characteristics from your lives and careers. Choose a conflict that turned out positively and discuss what characteristics were used that may have contributed to the outcome.

Next, choose a conflict that did not end well. Discuss how you might have used each characteristic to help create a better outcome. See the Key Terms for some reminders of how to use the five characteristics.

Chapter Summary

In this chapter, we looked at the mediator's job. A mediator is not a judge and should remain neutral. In addition, the mediator must be the person in control of all aspects of communication. Participants look to the mediator to guide the conversation to make sure there is balance of power, to provide a safe environment for open sharing, and to manage face. If a mediator does not exude confidence, the participants will get out of control or be uncomfortable participating. In chapter 4 we will take a more in-depth look at the structure of a mediation. This mediation model is used in countries all over the world. Regardless of culture, people are taught how to mediate in the same way. Why? Because it works!

Key Terms

Collaborative Communication helps the parties identify shared goals and priorities through a cooperative atmosphere to find common ground. Without establishing common ground, the likely result is reinforcement of the communication problems that created the conflict.

Face Management is an important mediation tool. "Saving face" is significant to participants and builds trust in the mediation process. No one likes to be embarrassed or humiliated.

Power Management is mediators bringing balance to each side by helping parties focus on their common goals. Modeling the behavior we'd like to see, treating everyone with respect, and being nonjudgmental are key elements in collaboration and ending power imbalances.

Process Management is guiding participants to focus on the "how" in discussing methods for communicating, making decisions, exploring differences, deliberating options, and agreeing on next steps.

Safe Environment provides both emotional and physical safety for everyone. Allowing people to choose where to sit can help participants feel more comfortable. Establishing guidelines about what type of communication is acceptable will help eliminate derogatory language. Communication and sharing are essential for a safe environment.

4

Basic Skills

Many trainers, writers, and teachers have delineated the stages of a mediation process. Whether consisting of seven steps, five steps, or four steps (as presented here), most agree that the stages of mediation are fluid, flexible, and part of a process. Mediation trainer Cynthia Olson believes that mediators need to be embedded in process. In fact, she points out that knowledge of the process is more important than content knowledge. When speaking of "leaning on the process," mediators trust these stages to bring the parties toward resolution. There are times when this process takes ten minutes (as when parties need five minutes of venting before they feel free to resolve) or many hours over several sessions (if issues are complicated and multifaceted or there are strong positional perspectives).

We like to think of mediation as passing through four stages:

1. Introduction
2. Storytelling
3. Problem solving
4. Resolution

These "stages" are helpful to give you an idea of how a typical mediation might flow, but we present them with some caveats. First, the stages are not usually distinct and separate. Often, they blend together or overlap. Second, not all mediations go through these stages in this order. Sometimes when you think you are in the problem-solving stage; you find that you must start storytelling all over. Third, the skills and processes we associate with a particular stage are never limited to that stage. You will find that you can use any of the skills at any stage in a mediation. The stages and their associated skills, then, are just a convenient way to learn mediation and not a picture of how any given case will unfold. *Always remember that there is no formula. Mediation is an art requiring constant judgment about how and when to intervene.*

Introduction

The introduction in a mediation session sets the tone for the rest of the process. Do not underestimate the importance of this step or leave it out in an effort to move forward quickly. If you forget some part of the stages, don't freak out; the session will provide multiple opportunities to recall important points. The introduction produces a little common ground—a point where the parties can start at the same place, despite their other differences. The introduction has three primary purposes—(1) to introduce the parties to the mediators and to each other; (2) to give an explanation of the process; and (3) to begin establishing trust.

In most cases, an "agreement to mediate" form has been given to the parties (see sample in the appendix). The conditions on this form must be agreed upon and signed by both parties. Usually, a signed form is required before moving forward with the process. Many mediators either memorize the different parts of the introduction or jot down the points on a note card to make sure they include everything they wish to cover.

Different mediators cover somewhat different things in their introductions. Some use a minimal introduction; others prefer a detailed presentation. The following parts of an introduction usually are included:

1. Introduction of mediators and parties
2. Words of encouragement

3. Explanation of the process and definitions of mediation and the mediator's role
4. Ground rules or communication guidelines
5. Confidentiality provisions
6. Caucus possibility
7. Signing the Agreement to Mediate
8. Asking for questions

A mediator needs to be flexible with these steps, as one of the parties may ask questions or make comments at any time. If the parties relate stories about previous mediations or begin explaining their current situation, the mediators should reassure them that they will have adequate time to explain, in a minute or two, but first they need to hear some necessary information.

The mediation relationship developed in the introduction helps the participants feel more comfortable and optimistic. If a trust relationship is created, the parties can participate openly while seeing the mediator as competent. All components of the introduction work together to set the tone and to establish trust. If a trusting environment is evident from the start, it will endure through the entire process. People often have misconceptions about mediation, and this is the time to get everyone on the same track. The following steps in the introduction all include trust-building methods.

Introduce Participants

When the parties first arrive, it is important to make introductions all around the table. Mediators usually inquire how the individuals would like to be addressed. A common response is to use first names. With a large group, it may be helpful to use name tags or write names on a board or a piece of paper. When mediators introduce themselves, it is helpful to fully describe their position: "I am Maria Lopez, a trained mediator with the Neighborhood Dispute Resolution Center. I am participating here as part of a contract with the Metro Court Mediation Program."

Offer Words of Encouragement

After everyone has introduced themselves, it is a good time to commend the participants for choosing to use the mediation process. Remind them that choosing to meet and discuss the dispute is a valuable first step. Just the fact that the parties are in attendance is positive movement toward resolution. These "complimentary" words can also be repeated throughout the process, whenever positive progress occurs. A mediator may occasionally give a process check-in with comments such as: "Wow, you have really made progress addressing your issues" or "I can see that last discussion was difficult for you, but you made your way through it."

Explain the Process

After the appropriate greetings and introductions take place, mediators need to explain the process of mediation as it will be used that day. This definition may include one of the following definitions or it may be a combination of several, as appropriate. You might explain, for example, that mediation is . . .

> . . . a collaborative process that focuses on individual interests and concerns, identifying options, testing expected consequences of those options, and allowing parties to see the perspective of the other;
>
> . . . a process where a neutral third party facilitates communication, so two parties have the opportunity to come up with a resolution that is mutually satisfactory;
>
> . . . a voluntary process where a mutually acceptable agreement is sought through the guidance of an impartial mediator team;
>
> . . . an interest-based process where a neutral third party facilitates negotiation;
>
> . . . a facilitated discussion of differences;
>
> . . . an opportunity for the parties to discuss their situation in a comfortable, productive way.

After defining the mediation process, it is important to explain the role the mediator plays. Often this is done by explaining what a mediator does *not* do: "We are neither judges nor arbiters. We will make no decisions for you nor give you advice toward resolving your problem. We will not take sides or advocate either side or position."

It is also helpful to explain what the mediator *does* do: "As impartial third parties, we will facilitate your communication and be in charge only of the process. We will help you discuss your problem with each other and guide you toward managing the problem." Trust can be built as mediators explain their role. The participants get their first glimpse of the impartiality of the mediator and begin to trust the process of mediation. A role we like to add when introducing ourselves, is to say we're "interpreters." When parties are in conflict, they often stop hearing one another. The mediator's job is to help you not only be heard but also to hear each other.

Ground Rules

After defining mediation and the role of the mediator, more common ground can be established by offering *ground rules* or *communication guidelines*. These guidelines revolve around the theme of "common courtesy." When mentioning courtesy in the process, a mediator is establishing a respectful atmosphere. Only one person should speak at a time, with no interruptions. Name calling or violent interjections and disturbances are not welcome in this process and may precipitate a break, a caucus (see discussion below), or an end to the session. To avoid interruptions, participants and mediators can take notes to remind themselves of a point they want to bring up later. Mediators can provide pencils and paper for this purpose.

There are different ideas among mediators about the role of ground rules. Some mediators are firm about establishing the rules right at the start. Others take a "wait-and-see" attitude. If an incident arises that needs attention, the mediators then ask the parties how they would like to deal with the situation. Still other mediators like to empower the participants early in the process. In our practice, we like to ask the parties in the introduction what they need in this session to help make the process as comfortable and constructive as possible. We find that when the parties participate in creating the ground rules, they are more likely to follow them or remind one another of them. If they mention that they would like respect, we can ask them to define respect ("What is respect to you?" "How would you know when you were respected?").

All participants need to be aware of time considerations. Someone may need to get back to work, catch a ride, or get to a childcare agency. In these cases, a mediator needs to make the parties aware of the options if mediation is cut short. Rescheduling should be an acceptable option. If that is not possible, participants can brainstorm about what they want to do if time runs out and the process is not finished. If the mediation does have a time limit, it is the mediator's responsibility to guide the process in a way that considers the time limit.

Confidentiality

There are different philosophies of confidentiality, and mediators have different opinions about it. You will need to know what standards of confidentiality you wish to follow or are required to follow by the program in which you are mediating. Most mediation programs today do not hold the parties to confidentiality, but they do require the mediators to keep the sessions private. If you sense that confidentiality may be an issue with either party, invite them to reach an agreement on how private they wish the session to be.

It is often the case, though not always, that the parties want to feel free to air their concerns without worrying about what an outsider might think if the particulars of the session were revealed. For example, participants might hesitate to criticize the work environment if they fear their statements will be repeated to managers of the company. Trust sets the stage for an environment conducive to creating an agreement that the parties are comfortable with and are willing to support. By keeping information about the mediation confidential, this safe atmosphere can be created. (See sample Agreement to Mediate, clause 5 in the appendix.) At a minimum, assure the parties that you will keep the session private. The mediator cannot be compelled to reveal to anyone the contents of a mediation session.

Caucus

Another point to be explained in the introduction is the possibility of calling a "caucus." These separate meetings are not always needed, but occasionally the parties reach an impasse, and the mediators decide to speak to each party individually. Let the parties know that you will spend equal time speaking with both of them. Otherwise, some parties may worry that you are biased or taking sides. Explaining the possibility of a caucus in your introduction is important, but if you forget you can always explain caucus when you ask for one. "I may have forgotten to tell you about a caucus earlier in my introduction, but I want to tell you about it now. I'd like to take a few minutes to meet with you each individually to clarify some things that will help me better guide our conversation." Some mediators use caucuses a great deal; others rarely call them. We think it is a good idea to tell the participants ahead of time about caucuses, just in case you find it necessary to have private meetings. The parties need to know, too, that they have the right to ask for a private meeting if they wish.

Sign the Agreement to Mediate

If you are working for a court program, you will probably be provided an "Agreement to Mediate" form or you can find a general one online enabling you to create your own. (See sample Agreement to Mediate in the appendix.) Be sure to give the participants a chance to read and understand this Agreement to Mediate. Review it with them if necessary. Answer their questions and have them sign the agreement. This is the first of many collaborative steps in the mediation. When both parties sign this form, they agree to its terms, which is a good start.

Ask for Questions

Before moving to the storytelling stage, it is important to ask if anyone has any questions or concerns. With a final smile of encouragement and acknowledgment that everyone is ready to begin, the mediators start the next stage.

EXERCISE

Part 1

Introduction Examples: Watch each mediation introduction below and then compare and contrast the following mediation introductions:

1. Is there one that stands out as more professional?
2. If you were a party in a mediation, which introduction would make you feel most comfortable?
3. Which introduction appeals to your potential style as a mediator?

MWI Opening Statement, Harvard Mediation Pedagogy Conference: https://youtu.be/xmZyztC9PCU

Landlord/Tenant Mediation: https://youtu.be/j6JEpg10pbw

Mediation: A Neighbor to Neighbor Conflict Role Play, The Mediation Process: https://youtu.be/KS-ykB7nYiY

Part 2

Every mediator has their own style of conducting a mediation as well as how they present their introduction, so speak in away that is comfortable to you. Take a few minutes to write a basic introduction. Make sure to include the parts of an introduction mentioned earlier. Next, in groups of two, take turns practicing your mediation introduction and giving one another feedback as to what worked well and what could be improved. Use notes to remind yourself about all the components to be discussed.

Storytelling Stage

This phase of the mediation process is sometimes called the "information gathering" or "fact finding" period. For some, it seems similar to the opening statements in a court hearing. Each party is invited to give an "opening statement." However, we prefer a different framing, which is why we use the term *sto-*

rytelling. Each party has a chance to discuss their view of what happened, is happening, or could happen in the future. Often the parties will "make a case" similar to the one they would make in court. Other times, they just want to vent. Sometimes, too, the parties identify the problem or suggest a solution. Often the mediators ask the person who brought the case to mediation to speak first. Other times the mediators will arbitrarily choose someone to go first. We usually just ask the participants how they would like to start. Here are some helpful ways you might begin this stage:

> "Let's begin by having each of you describe what you feel is the crux of the problem. Both of you will have the same opportunity, so please don't interrupt to state your position."
>
> "Tell us what brought you to mediation."
>
> "What is the problem you are confronting?"
>
> "What is happening?"

Student's Journal Entry

I had never thought about how the telling and re-telling of a story helps participants clarify their needs as they listen to each refinement of their story and sift out what's nonessential.

The participants can be reminded that it would be helpful simply to describe or explain the situation—not to accuse or confront. If the parties interrupt or break the ground rules, the mediators can remind them to take notes concerning what they want to say and to reassure them that they will have their turn to speak. Sometimes it is useful to encourage the parties to direct their speaking to the mediators, rather than to each other. This can help reduce anger or tension. At other times, it is constructive for the parties to talk directly with one another. One indicator that the mediation is headed in a positive direction is when the parties stop talking to the mediator and start talking with one another. This can indicate they are feeling more comfortable and leaning toward a potential agreement.

While the parties are explaining their stories, the mediator needs to watch and listen carefully. This is the time to begin noting positions and interests. Verbal and nonverbal behavior can give lots of information to aid the process. For example, the mediator can listen to how a participant characterizes the problem. Are they dividing the issue into an "us" versus "them" conflict? Does the vocabulary indicate a lack of emotional control? Does the participant portray themselves as a victim? How much eye contact is there between the two parties or with the mediator? What does the body posture indicate? Submission? Defiance? Does each party listen to the other, or does one or both scribble notes furiously at the first statement made? What word(s) triggered the response?

Often the parties' stories contradict one another. Avoid the temptation to figure out who is correct. This is not your job as a mediator. Instead, treat each story respectfully and realize that different people naturally will have different versions of what happened. An important part of storytelling is for the parties to hear one another's perspective and to learn significant new things. Let that happen.

Ideally, the length of speaking time should be balanced for each party's opening statement. Five to ten minutes each can give parties enough time to present a picture of the problem. If one party seems to be taking too long, the mediator can courteously ask them to summarize. The mediator also may want to intervene politely and try to summarize for that person by saying, "You have given a lot of good information. What I heard you say that is most important to you is . . . Does that sound correct?" Your ability to summarize constructively will improve as you practice mediation. You want to allow a party to share their position but not allow them to dominate time or the mediation. If one party does not say much, the mediator can encourage the person to tell more of the story by asking, "What happened next?" "How did that make you feel?" "Tell me more about what happened."

It is essential for the mediator to remember how important these opening statements are. Often it is only after being given the opportunity to share their *whole* story that parties feel comfortable enough to continue the process. The following listening techniques let the parties know that their stories *are* important.

To find common ground, right from the start the mediator listens for the commonalties the parties value or find important. The mediator makes brief notes about these commonalities on their personal notepad or possibly on a flip chart labeled "common ground." In times of impasse or argument, the mediator is able to remind the parties what they have in common to shift the focus from areas of disagreement. Pointing out common ground also helps the parties see that they may be closer to a resolution than they realize. The following video clip is edited from the movie *Wedding Crashers* and offers a humorous look at the use of finding common ground and summarizing: https://youtu.be/1X3AtSDFrYo.

> ***Student's Journal Entry***
>
> Mediation goes so much better when the "problem" is not the focus. It is so destructive when mediators approach stories as testimony.

Listening Techniques

The listening techniques used in the storytelling stage also should be used throughout the rest of the process. The purpose of these techniques in this stage is to let the participants know that both their feelings and the substance of the issue are valid entities to be considered. The mediators are showing respect for the parties, which in turn builds trust in the mediators and in the process.

Listening is an *active* (rather than passive) process, and mediators should attempt to understand the emotions expressed, the substance (facts) of the problem, and what the positions and interests are. Mediators do this by being active participant observers. Attentive posture and respectful eye communication are important indicators of involvement. Mediators can nod their heads, say "uh-huh," and use facial expressions that show an attitude of caring and concern.

While inaccurate perceptions, faulty assumptions, and distractions affect how well we receive incoming messages, there can also be a physical reason for difficulty in listening. Wolvin and Coakley (1992) found that people have spare time to use when they are listening. The average person speaks between 125 and 150 words per minute, while most humans are capable of understanding speech at rates of as many as 500 words per minute. While it is easy to lose concentration during this extra time, mediators can use it to understand the speaker's ideas and to read the nonverbal signals. Without effective listening, the mediator will be unable to summarize, clarify, reframe, and acknowledge elements learned in the introduction and storytelling stages of the mediation process.

EXERCISE **"Active Listening"**

In a group setting, brainstorm topics of discussion to find one that would ensure a lively discussion. When the group has chosen a topic that everyone knows something about, one person begins with their perspective on that issue. Other participants cannot give their opinion or perspective until they have accurately summarized the previous person's message. Take care to reflect emotions and feelings as well as to reframe the substance or facts of the message. When summarizing a message, it is important to check with the first speaker to determine if the summary was accurate. If not, some clarification may be needed. Go around the group until each participant has summarized the person before them and given their own perspective.

Restating

Restating simply means paraphrasing or repeating something one of the participants said. Restating can be helpful in showing that you are listening, repeating an important point for everyone to hear, or acknowledging something a person feels is important. It is also a way to check to make sure that you understood the speaker's point. Restating may sound simple, or even obvious, but participants do appreciate when a mediator seems to have heard what they said. When a mediator restates what one participant says, it is shared with everyone at the table–a safe way to express important information. As in the following example, a restatement can include some or all of the original wording.

> Participant: "I am so disgusted when my partner leaves the kitchen a mess."
>
> Mediator: "You are disgusted when the kitchen is a mess."

Summarizing

Summarizing is a kind of restatement, but it usually includes several points. After each opening statement, it is helpful for mediators to summarize what they have heard. The important issues and facts can be pulled together at this point, establishing a common ground before further discussion ensues. A mediator can begin summarizing statements this way:

> "It sounds like the three main issues you are concerned with are . . ."
>
> "Let's see if I have this straight; you experienced______ and feel ______."
>
> "Let me summarize what I've heard so far."

These statements can produce a basis for further discussion, especially when the participants correct the mediator's assumptions. If a participant does not agree with the summarization, further storytelling may be needed.

Summarizing also is a useful tool to review progress in the session. Participants usually like to feel that they are getting somewhere and that this problem-statement period is leading somewhere. Mediators can review progress with statements such as:

> "You've decided that ______ and ______are not huge problem areas to be dealt with, so let us move on to . . ."

"It looks like each of you has gotten a lot of new information on this issue. You have a clearer picture of the choices before you. Here's what I see that they are."

Summarizing is a way to highlight the important points for the participants and the mediator. Mediators often summarize periodically throughout the whole session to tie together the main points of the story that have surfaced. Even when nearing resolution, it is helpful to summarize the progression thus far in identifying the facts. Participants see this as another respectful measure of assurance that the mediators are concerned with the whole story.

Asking Questions

After the opening statements, which are mostly monologues, the process becomes more of an exchange between the participants and the mediators. At this stage, the mediator has heard about the events that precipitated the dispute, and the participants are responding to issues brought up in the opening statements.

The mediator may still need to get more information on specific issues and can often ask questions to clarify:

"I'd like some more information about what happened after the incident. Could you share more?"

"John, how do you respond to Jane's statement that you . . .?"

"Pete, can you tell me more about . . .?"

Mediators must be careful not to appear to be judging the participants or the events. The mediator's questions need to be specific and to the point, keeping the discussion on the issues in question. Obviously, questions like "How can you have hurt your husband like that?" or "That certainly is not a fair business deal, is it?" can provoke defensiveness in the participants.

The type of question influences the process in different ways. *Closed questions* are those that elicit a "yes," "no," or one-word answer. These questions are useful for confirming a mediator's summarization or establishing a specific point of fact for both parties to acknowledge. These questions are not preferred when exploring an issue for more information. Instead, *open questions* seek more information and invite longer answers. Beginning a question with words like "how" or "what" or "why" (exercising caution so that these statements don't sound accusatory) will encourage more details and more precise identification of the problem. There is sometimes a need to be careful of "why" questions. They may evoke defensiveness in the participants, who could think that the mediator is asking for justification of actions. The "why" of a question could be inserted further into the statement, such as, "I'd like some more information as to why you are feeling that way." When mediators use clarifying tools, they are implying that what has been said has value. Besides stating to participants that they are concerned with the whole story, mediators model a quest for clear information about both facts and feelings.

Reframing

Reframing involves restating what a person said with a slightly different perspective. Reframing improves communication between the parties and helps mediators check on the actual intended message. Reframing also puts the message into language that may be easier for the other party and mediators to understand. When mediators reframe, they let the speaker know that they grasp the facts. By restating the basic ideas, mediators put the message into easy-to-understand language, such as, "In other words, what happened is . . ." or "So, your idea is to . . ."

Some more specific ways that mediators use reframing are to:

- *Identify commonalities*—"I see you are both interested in security."
- *Increase or decrease the level of emotion*—"It looks like you have some extremely strong feelings about dishonesty."
- *Bring out the interests beneath the positions*—"I recognize that you want to make money and secure your reputation."

Using a technique that redefines an issue, mediators can help the process move toward resolution. When possible, try to paraphrase with a positive twist.

> Participant: "Jim is always late, strolling in like it doesn't affect the rest of us!"

Our first inclination may be to paraphrase as follows. Mediator: "So, you don't like that Jim is always late?" This doesn't sound like a bad paraphrase, however it's possible Jim may become upset and believe that even the mediator is against him. A positive paraphrase would be something like this: "What I'm hearing is that you value timeliness?" Again, restate/paraphrase with a positive spin. As parties see the issues more clearly and begin to note commonalities, they are inclined to have confidence in and to continue the process.

Reflecting

One strength of the mediation process is attention to the emotional or feeling component in a dispute or conflict. Many models of conflict management put effort only into dealing with the content (facts, evidence). Mediation encourages exploration of the feelings associated with the conflict.

A tool that mediators use to convey the message that emotions are an important part of the process is *reflection of feelings*. By listening to the feelings (stated or implied) underlying the content, mediators can echo the emotions and check to see if their impressions are accurate. Reflection of feelings can occur at any stage in the process. One participant tells the following story:

> My daughter continually shuts me out of her life. Every time I try to talk to her, she either walks away or gives me a dirty look. I have begged her to talk to me, bribed her with new clothes, and ordered her to be more respectful. She just hates me!

Mediators can respond to just the feelings, giving a reflection: "It sounds like you are frustrated with your daughter's behavior," or "You really would like to be respected by your daughter," or even "You are really frustrated." Alternatively, they could give a more direct restatement: "You want your daughter to talk to you and not shut you out." Whichever reflection is used, it is important for mediators to signal either verbally or nonverbally that this is a perception and invite the participant to confirm, deny, or clarify the perception. Mediators can pause with a questioning look or ask, "Did I perceive that correctly?" By letting the parties know that these reflections are a search for accurate information about how this problem makes them feel, mediators show respect and concern for the disputants. These statements encourage parties to take responsibility for

Student's Journal Entry

Venting is something I do very well. I love to talk. In conflict, I always assumed that if I was doing all of the talking, then I must be winning. Nothing could be further from the truth. All I was doing by not letting the other person speak was drowning out other opinions. All that achieved was to harden or worsen perceptions of me as a bully—I wasn't "winning," I was losing all opportunity to improve the situation and was creating more obstacles.

EXERCISE **"Reflecting Feelings"**

In dyads, one person picks a word (privately) from the following list and tells of an instance that evoked that feeling. The other person responds by looking at the list and selecting the feeling. Start out the reflections with statements like: "It sounds like you're feeling . . ." "I hear you . . ." "You are feeling . . ." After each reflection, the listener needs to check that the identified feeling is the correct one by pausing and waiting for a clarification or asking, "Have I described your feelings correctly?"

Angry	Enthusiastic	Inhibited	Shaky
Bitter	Excited	Intimidated	Surprised
Bored	Fearful	Irritable	Suspicious
Comfortable	Frustrated	Lukewarm	Tense
Concerned	Grateful	Miserable	Terrified
Content	Helpless	Mixed up	Trapped
Devastated	High	Nervous	Uneasy
Disgusted	Hurt	Puzzled	Vulnerable
Disturbed	Hopeful	Resentful	Weak
Embarrassed	Humiliated	Sad	Worried
Empty			

their feelings and to correct the mediators if the perception is wrong. Other reflecting statements include, "You *seem* to be feeling miserable because John refuses to pay you the debt," or "It *sounds* like you are puzzled by the behavior of your boss at the staff meeting."

Sometimes it is helpful to practice adding "emotion" words to a listener's vocabulary to be prepared for this active listening. By increasing the number of words that describe feeling, we can help ourselves and others more correctly identify emotions and what lies behind them.

Acknowledging

Throughout the entire mediation process, mediators can validate or encourage the parties by commending their efforts or confirming that what was said was heard. This can include acknowledging feelings or emotions, "I can see you are upset/angry/frustrated; can you tell me what is going on?" A common place for acknowledgment is at the beginning of each session—as mentioned earlier in the chapter. When progress or movement is noted, a mediator can say, "Conflict management is hard work . . . you're doing great!" After particularly intense emotions, an acknowledgement could be, "I understand how difficult this must be for you . . . you're doing fine." As the process is nearing resolution, mediators can say, "You've both worked so hard! We are almost ready to write an agreement."

Mediators can continue to use certain phrases and a positive tone of voice to encourage the parties to keep talking. For example, phrases like "That is interesting" and "Yes, I see" help move the process along and also model effective listening skills. Listeners who acknowledge the speaker's message convey their own message of encouragement and respect. Acknowledgement is a mediation tool that we can use in everyday life, "Wow, you look great in that outfit!" or "You seem sad today." Acknowledging a person's feelings or emotions is not about agreeing with them, rather it is about "seeing" them. Tone and content affect how we react to the rest of any conversation.

EXERCISE **"World's Biggest Eye Contact Experiment"**

Watch the following video, then partner up and try the exercise. It will be difficult and awkward at first but the power of being "seen" and acknowledged is powerful and transcends culture.

https://youtu.be/3QdnCRWATZ8

Problem-Solving Stage

In the storytelling stage, the parties have explained their positions and interests, and the mediators have begun to clarify the problem by identifying the issues and emotions of both parties. In the problem-solving stage, the conflict at hand (often called a "dispute") will be clearly defined, a crucial step in the mediation process. Often, the issues are presented as positions, sounding like demands or offers. Mediators can help to sort out the issues so that each party's interests can be explored, moving the parties away from positions. Next, an agenda will be set, and options will be generated and evaluated.

EXERCISE **"Interests Underlying Positions"**

Write down five of your most strongly held positions. For each of these positions, list three or four possible interests, principles, and/or values that contributed to forming that position. Note the primary interest that truly motivates you to hold the position. (Be aware that others may attribute your position to other interests.)

If the mediation gets to a problem-solving stage, we recommend the four components presented by Roger Fisher and William Ury (1991) in *Getting to Yes: Negotiating Agreement without Giving In*. Fisher and Ury use a strategy developed at the Harvard Negotiation Project called *principled negotiation* where issues are decided on their merits while looking for mutual gains. The following four principles (introduced in chapter 1) comprise this method of problem solving:

> *Separate the people from the problem*—When two parties are very positional (that is, having predetermined a particular stance) in their view of the conflict, the relationship and the content of the conflict often get confused. It is important to separate the people (relationship, personalities) from the problem (facts, content, substance). Deal with the people as human beings and deal with the problem on its merits.

> *Focus on interests, not positions*—The interests behind positions are the needs, desires, concerns, and fears that caused the party to adopt that position. Often, behind seemingly incompatible positions one finds shared interests. By reconciling interests, rather than compromising on positions, a mutually advantageous solution can result. The following example illustrates the importance of determining interests. Two siblings were fighting over the last orange in the fruit basket. Their mother could have made a quick decision either to split the orange or to give the orange to the child who had the cleanest room or who had been the most respectful that day. If the mother had taken a minute to explore *why* each child wanted the orange, she may have found that they had compatible interests. One child wanted the peel of the orange to feed the hamster, and the other wanted a snack. Compatible interests often lie beneath seemingly incompatible positions.

> *Invent options for mutual gain*—When two parties are negotiating, they often have the assumption of a "fixed pie." The perception is that there is only a certain amount of "pie" (time, finances, assets, resources), and if one wins or gets more, the other loses or gets less. The principle suggested here is to assume a larger pie. Negotiators can expand the pie by inventing options before dividing it. This creative expansion can produce a much larger range of options with benefits for each side.

Insist on using objective criteria—When settling differences in positions and interests, it is often important to look at solutions on the basis of objective criteria, independent of either side. This approach encourages the parties to commit themselves to reaching a solution based on principle, not pressure. By accepting fair standards and methods of testing the reality of options, a fair and acceptable outcome results.

Student's Journal Entry

The problem is that both sides are so locked into their positions that it is hard to imagine them committing to any joint problem-solving process. They had reached a so-called compromise, but that offered only a stopgap, temporary halt to the conflict. The compromise did not address the needs of either party. No one was committed to it, and neither side paid any attention to it.

Issue Framing

An issue is simply a point of disagreement, and many conflicts will have several issues. Issues can focus on content (facts, money, contracts) or procedures (method of payment, dispute resolution process, time constraints, and a host of other topics). Normally, people in a conflict will state their issues in terms of opposing positions: I want this, you want that. One of the many ways that mediators can be helpful is to guide the participants in a process of framing their issues constructively. In the problem-solving stage, you want to frame issues as open, non-judgmental questions that invite the parties to solve the problem for mutual gain.

Think of an issue statement as a question requiring a creative solution, something to the effect of "What shall we do?" or "What are our options?" or "How can we solve this problem?" Here are some examples:

Situation: James and Mary, a married couple, work in different parts of town. Normally, James takes the car to work, and Mary takes the bus. Mary complains that the bus is inconvenient and unpleasant and wants the car. James says he must get to work on time and has a greater need for the car than Mary.

Conflict framing: Who will get the car, James or Mary?

Problem framing: What can James and Mary do to meet both of their transportation needs?

Situation: The Thomas's dog bit the Smiths' son. The Smiths say that the dog is mean and should be put to sleep. The Thomases say that their dog is not mean and that the Smiths' son teased the dog and hit it with a stick. They say that the dog should not be put to sleep.

Conflict framing: Should the dog be put to sleep or not?

Problem framing: What should the Smiths and Thomases do to ensure a safe play environment for children in the neighborhood?

Situation: A customer returned a blouse to the cleaners, claiming that they ruined it. She said that she does not have enough money to buy a new blouse and wants the cleaners to pay for a new one. The cleaners say that the blouse was damaged before it came in and that they should not be responsible for replacing the blouse.

Conflict framing: Should the cleaners pay for the blouse or not?

Problem framing: What can the cleaners and customer do to help the customer deal with her loss while also maintaining good customer relations for the store?

As mediators help disputants frame their issues as problem questions, they tune the parties in to their essential interests and move them toward creative problem solving.

However, positions are often presented as "bottom lines," and it is sometimes difficult for the parties to see how their two incompatible positions can ever be reconciled. This is why people often reach an impasse. If, however, they can make the shift from thinking in terms of positions to thinking about interests, they will be ready to frame their issues in a new way that will turn the conflict into a problem-solving collaboration.

In a family mediation, a mother and a teenage son are discussing a proposed curfew. The position of the mother is that she wants her son home at 10:00 every night. The son's position is that he thinks the curfew is too early, and he wants to stay out until midnight. A search for interests in this situation may reveal the mother's interest in her son's safety, her own fear about being home alone at night, and maybe even fear of losing control of her son. The son may be interested in retaining independence or maintaining a reputation. Issues may emerge concerning content (what the son does from 10:00 to 12:00; why the mother is so afraid) or as procedural (the son is not willing to explore options; the mother has to get back to work soon; or the father is a necessary third party to help them to complete agreements).

As the issues and interests are being identified, mediators need to help the parties clearly see the delineation and the connections. Use of a flip chart, blackboard, or paper to record the lists gives people a better picture of all the motivating factors beneath their positions. The following techniques assist mediators in making the transition from positions to interests:

- Focus on interests rather than positions; ask "Why does that concern you?"
- Go beyond positions; ask "What makes that position desirable?"
- Avoid focusing on or asking about preferred outcomes too early in the process.
- Identify and emphasize common interests and mutual gains—"I am hearing you both state that the safety of the children is a primary concern."
- Generate and promote creative and multiple options in order to obtain a fair solution for all. Guiding principle: separate the people from the problem.

Point out common ground, which can show the parties they are closer to a potential resolution than they think.

A caveat: Most mediators will tell you that collaborative problem solving is better than positional bargaining, but the latter is often the simpler way to go. Indeed, if the parties would rather just compromise and find an acceptable position in the middle and they are able to do so, let them. This is often how mediation proceeds, and it is not the mediator's role to judge that. On the other hand, if they are headed toward impasse and unable to transcend the conflict, you may want to encourage them to frame their issues more creatively and constructively, as described above.

EXERCISE **"Positions and Interests"**

For each of the three issues in conflict, list and discuss the following:

1. The position of Chris
   The position of Pat
2. Two interests of Chris
   Two interests of Pat
3. Reframe the issue to include both of their interests.

Issues:

a. Pat and Chris are in the library, disagreeing about whether a window nearby should be open or closed.
b. Pat and Chris are discussing distribution of household chores in their home. They are in disagreement over who needs to take the trash out on Wednesdays.
c. Pat is a teacher and wants Chris transferred out of the classroom. They disagree about the transfer.

Agenda Setting

At some point, it may be desirable to set an agenda or prioritize concerns before exploring the options. Here you will summarize the issues you believe are important to the parties, check to see if you depicted those issues accurately, and work with the parties to put the issues into a logical order. This agenda setting occurs *after* storytelling but *before* option generation or discussions about agreements (discussed below). The parties can state their preference about which issue to discuss first, and if they disagree, they can negotiate a starting point. Mediators sometimes suggest starting with an issue that is nearing resolution or has common interests. By beginning with an easy issue, a conciliatory mood can be set, and the parties can experience trust in the process.

On the other hand, participants can choose to start with the most important issue, especially if it seems to be overriding all else. Whichever order is chosen, mediators need to check with both parties to see if they are in agreement. It may be helpful to write the agenda on a flip chart, blackboard, or paper. The agenda discussion should address whether one meeting is sufficient for the issues identified. If more than one meeting is required, the agenda can target how much should be accomplished in each meeting. This may be a good time to discuss time constraints with the participants so that schedules can be coordinated and the proper amount of time allotted to address complex issues conveniently for all parties.

A mediator can help sort things out by leading an agenda-setting process. Agenda setting is especially helpful when the conflict is complex and involves many, somewhat separate issues. The participants themselves may feel confused about how to begin unraveling what looks like a large tangle and will be relieved when the mediator helps them simplify it.

Agenda setting is not always a good idea. If the issues are related to one another and creative solutions lie in linking one issue with another, you may prefer to let things remain a bit

Words of the Wise

In most people's minds, inventing simply is not part of the negotiating process. People see their job as narrowing the gap between positions, not broadening the options available. They tend to think, "We're having a hard-enough time agreeing as it is. The last thing we need is a bunch of different ideas." By looking from the outset for the single best answer, you are likely to short circuit a wiser decision-making process in which you select from a large number of possible answers.

—Roger Fisher and William Ury (p. 61)

complex, at least for the moment. Alternatively, you could decide to summarize the issues but not discuss them separately. After agenda setting, you are ready to begin generating options to address the issues.

Let us say, for example, that a worker and employer are mediating an employment contract. The issues turn out to be salary, benefits, work space, computer equipment, and safety. If you try to "solve" these one at a time, you may "force" the parties into positional compromises rather than interest-based problem solving. Here are some potential solutions that arise by discussing the issues together rather than separately:

- A lower salary in return for a new computer.
- Moving the work space to another, safer location.
- Higher benefits in return for lower salary.
- New furniture and office appointments of the employee's choice instead of a computer upgrade.

Student's Journal Entry

Creative options would be an excellent way to start thinking at the grade school level. Maybe we might have a chance of stopping the noneffective ways we look for everyday answers.

Option Generation

With a well-framed issue and a clear picture of each party's interests and their common ground, mediators can guide the parties in exploring options. This step in the problem-solving stage can be powerful if separated into three parts: reviewing interests, brainstorming options, and evaluating options.

Mediators begin this stage by focusing again on the interests that have been expressed in previous stages. Allow time to review once more what each party needs from an agreement *before* looking for solutions. Concerning the issue at hand, a mediator can say, "I see that John needs _______ and Manuel needs _______.If we are able to achieve a solution that meets those interests, would you be satisfied?" Although there is a chance this may lead to more exploration of interests, it is helpful to check once more for a clear picture of the interests before moving on.

The second part of option generation is the brainstorming step. This can be initiated by a simple question to each participant, "How do we resolve this?" or one that directly addresses the issue, "What does it mean to be a good neighbor?" Mediators can more formally invite the parties to brainstorm: "I'd like each of you (or both of you together) to brainstorm a list of possible solutions to this problem. Let's be very creative here with all ideas welcomed. Please hold your comments on the options until later when we will evaluate each one. Remember, these are possible ideas, not offers that you will be held to." Separating the generating of options from the evaluating of options is a powerful tool that can prevent premature judging that inhibits brainstorming. The mediator should write down each idea with equal verbal and nonverbal gestures. If verbal comments are made, they also should treat each suggestion equally. We don't want to indicate our approval of one suggestion over another.

At this point, mediators may bring up an offer or solution that was introduced by the parties earlier in the mediation. These may need to be repeated to reflect the interests and ideas the parties have identified: "If I remember correctly, you mentioned earlier that you were interested in safety in your neighborhood and suggested _______."

Role-reversal is a mediation technique that stretches the parties' creativity. Invite one party to suggest a solution that would meet the other's needs and vice versa: "Manuel, if you were a car-repair business owner like John, what would you do to ensure customer safety in the parking lot?"

The brainstorming step expands possibilities for resolution, or "expands the pie." With no judgments or evaluations yet, participants feel comfortable to think beyond positions and explore how interests can be met.

EXERCISE **"Thinking Out of the Box: Connect the Dots"**

Make sixteen (16) dots on a piece of paper—four groups of four in a square. Using four connecting lines, cover each dot. Try every possible solution. What does this have to do with mediation?

The last part of the option generation step is to evaluate the options. Mediators call this "reality testing" or "reality checking." Mediators use the list of interests generated earlier as the objective criteria for judging the efficacy of the solutions suggested. Questions are asked to make sure each option is one parties can live with. The goal is to determine if the options are fair, clear, and realistic. Mediators should probe perceptions of the parties—remembering that fairness and clearness are from the disputants' perspectives, not the mediator's! When checking if the option is realistic, mediators can ask questions like "If this option were put into place, how would it work?" "Will this option meet both of your needs?" "How will this solution affect you?" "Can you afford these payments?" "Will this schedule fit your workday?" "Will this meet Chris's interest for _______ and Juan's interest for _______?"

Tools for Deliberation

When the parties talk about each option in some detail and weigh the pros and cons in terms of their interests, they are deliberating well. Many conflict management processes begin with arguments: "Here's why I'm right and you're wrong!" If a mediation goes well, however, the parties will begin to move to a different kind of talk: They will begin to frame their issues in a new way, generate options, and deliberate collaboratively. This does not mean that they will suddenly agree on every point, but they will be empowered to say what is important to them and acknowledge one another's perspectives and interests. When they reach this point, there are several things you can do to help them weigh the options and move toward an acceptable solution. Here we describe two that we especially like.

Yes, No, Interesting. Once a list of options is generated, the parties can go back and discuss each one. You can even have each disputant vote on each option—"Yes," meaning I am willing to accept it; "No," meaning I am unwilling to accept it; or "Interesting," meaning let's talk about it more. Write each person's "vote" next to the option and you can quickly see what might be included in an agreement and what might be discussed further. Go back to each point marked "Interesting" by one or more of the parties and have them talk about what makes that interesting to them. Here they can explore creative ideas without committing to anything.

Concerns-Visions-Actions. The CVA model is an excellent way to achieve constructive conversation on a difficult topic. People who have differences concerning a common issue usually have concerns about the issue, a vision for their preferred future, and actions that would create that vision and address those concerns. Spend a little time having the parties talk about their concerns, what troubles them, and what problems they see. Next, have them talk about their visions, or what things would be like once the conflict is resolved. Finally, have them talk about the actions that they might take to achieve their visions. You may decide that you do not want to work CVA in this order. Maybe you want them to start on a positive note by discussing their visions first, moving to actions second. Or maybe they want to discuss actions first and then talk about their visions—how things will be different once these actions are taken.

After a good period of problem solving, using these methods or others, both the mediators and the parties are anxious to be done. You may feel tempted to rush through the final stages. Slow things down to assure a lasting and workable agreement is achieved. Considering long- and short-term implications helps test the option: "This sounds good to you today, but will it work for you a year from now?" If it seems that one of the parties has caved in or given up, mediators can carefully check with them: "Earlier you stated that you would never agree to pay $500; I'm wondering what has changed now?"

If, after a thorough evaluation of all options, the parties feel there are no options on which they can agree, they can take some comfort in the knowledge that they have thoroughly explored all possibilities. Parties should be commended on the hard work of brainstorming and evaluating options. They should have a much better picture of each other's interests, and that picture can impact their future relationship even without a mediated agreement. This outcome can be an acceptable resolution to them.

When parties reach a mutually acceptable resolution, the mediation process can seem like "magic." Sometimes the magic doesn't materialize, and parties cannot reach agreement. They may actively decide that they do not want to reach an agreement. Perhaps they feel it would be in their best interest to live with the conflict, ignore it, or even take it to court.

Mediations should not be evaluated in terms of agreement or "solving the problem." Instead, mediations should be seen as an opportunity for the parties to make good, clear decisions about the situation they face. A mediation in which the parties have a constructive conversation and decide jointly not to reach an agreement is far better than one in which the parties rush to an ill-conceived and unsatisfactory solution without having talked constructively and tested their interests.

Student's Journal Entry

In mediation and negotiation, agreements for the sake of agreement tend to lead to disappointment. It is important that disputants be clear about what their interests are and be persistent in seeing that the agreement is one that they can support.

Resolution Stage

The option-exploration process should reveal, at a minimum, commonalities. Ideally, it will point to compatible solutions. Mediators are now ready to help parties form an agreement that is satisfactory to them both. More questions start the agreement-writing stage: "Now that you've agreed on these two options, how do we make a resolution incorporating them?" Make sure that all the points both parties feel are important are included in the agreement. The agreement needs to have balance, with suggestions for resolution coming from each of the participants.

Most agreement forms have spaces for dates, names of all parties, signatures, and lines to write the agreement. Some mediators write the agreement on a separate sheet of paper and type up the agreement later to be sent to both sides. Other mediators write the agreements at the table, using the disputants' own words. Whichever method of agreement writing is chosen, it is important to make sure the parties are agreeing to what is being written. Further reality testing can go on here, checking if the terms are workable and actually solve the problem. Make sure the most minute details are written down, not leaving any room for disagreements: "Who is going to pay for the fence?" "How high will the fence be?" "What color will the fence be painted?"

Before the final signatures are given, mediators need to offer a last opportunity to ask questions or make comments. This is another place to watch for nonverbal signals of discomfort from the parties. Displays of continued anger or resentment may signal discomfort with the agreement. Behaviors such as head in hands or staring at the wall could mean parties are resigned to an agreement they don't want. Tears, fidgeting, or other signs of nervousness may need to be clarified with careful questions. Although it would be hard to discontinue writing the agreement at this point, it is better to end the mediation than to have the parties agree to something with which they are not happy.

Other reasons for not writing an agreement may include:

1. Hesitancy to put agreements in writing, not trusting confidentiality
2. Parties need more information; they want to postpone a final agreement until after talking with a boss, a spouse, etc.
3. Strong entrenchment in positions, unable to move toward interest-based negotiating
4. Preference to settle matter in court

Even the best-intentioned people sometimes cannot or do not reach a win/win solution. After all, there are some pies that have a limited number of pieces (number of children, amount of money, time available). The desire to learn what the other person wants and the effort to satisfy those desires can build a climate of collaboration that can do some preventive work for the future of their relationship. Mediators need to remember that they are there to manage the process, not to save relationships or to heal an unhealthy business deal. By participating in the mediation process and observing the skills modeled by the mediator, people learn to assess their interests and to see how to participate in interest-based negotiations.

Student's Journal Entry

One party plainly refused to sign anything, no matter what was written or agreed upon. This sense of stubbornness and paranoia was impossible for me to work around and still remain neutral.

The final minutes of the mediation process will include handing out copies of the agreement, handshakes, and some last commendations for choosing a process that allows the parties to participate in managing their own disputes. It is important to remain "in neutral" until the parties have left the room. Sometimes, a party will remain after the mediation in an attempt to discuss the case with the mediators. Mediators need to remain impartial, stating they were there as process managers with no interest in the terms or content.

Often after a session, mediators feel it is helpful to "debrief" with other mediators concerning the session. This is a time for discussion of the ups and downs of the process, including evaluation and suggestions that would have helped the process move more smoothly. Conflict situations can be emotional and stressful, and this informal time can relieve stress for the mediators and prepare them for the next mediation.

> ***Student's Journal Entry***
>
> My first real mediation! All of the stuff actually works when put to the test. Whenever we came to an impasse, I remembered another idea learned from role plays or scenarios. I found that role reversals really worked well. There was a lot of tension between the parties because they knew they would have to face each other at work after the session.

Chapter Summary

There are many techniques that a mediator uses to guide parties through what can be difficult conversations. While reaching a resolution may seem ideal, it may not happen—and that's okay. The most important result of the mediation could be simply the participants having a productive conversation. The process begins with the mediator's opening statement. The introduction should be honed over time so that it encompasses all necessary elements and feels natural. This sets the tone for the entire mediation, gives guidelines for behaviors, and builds trust in the competency of mediator. The parties gain an understanding of what to expect and what the mediation will entail.

There is no formula for a perfect mediation, but remembering the stages is key to the process. For example, participants have reached the resolution stage when someone suddenly reverts to storytelling. The mediators are the guide but need to remember the process belongs to the disputants. Don't rush the process and you will have a more successful outcome!

Key Terms

Acknowledging is validating or encouraging the parties by commending their efforts or confirming that what was said was heard.

Active Listening is giving appropriate verbal responses and nonverbal cues that tell the parties they are being heard and understood.

Caucus is a separate meeting with each party, often used to help the mediator understand an issue that might not be appropriate to discuss with the other party present.

Confidentiality means everything said in the mediation stays in the room. An agreement is the only part of a mediation that would not remain confidential.

Ground Rules are guidelines the mediator and participants create together that revolve around the theme of "common courtesy" and how the mediation should proceed.

Interests are what we need or what is important to us in an outcome.

Introduction is the first step of the mediation, which sets the tone and gives a general overview of what the process will be.

Issue Framing is when a mediator takes a point of disagreement and turns it into a question requiring a creative solution.

Positions are the outcomes we want to achieve.

Reflection (of feelings) is when a mediator echoes the emotions of the participants and check to see if their impressions are accurate. This can occur at any stage in the process.

Reframing is when the mediator restates what a person said with a slightly different (positive) perspective. Reframing improves communication between the parties and helps mediators confirm the intended message.

Restating is when a mediator paraphrases or repeats what a participant has said.

Storytelling is the stage of the mediation where the participants tell their side of the story and why they came to mediation.

Summarizing is when the mediator restates several points the parties have made to ensure clarity.

5

The Communication Perspective

Someone has to break the cycle. Albert Einstein is generally credited with having said, "The definition of insanity is doing the same thing over and over again and expecting different results." Although we understand this in theory, our logic tends to go out the window when we are in conflict and inevitably we end up doing just that. Why? Because most people don't want to back down. Even those who favor avoidance don't break the cycle by not participating. And yet, in order to get what we want or what we need, we need to do something differently. In this chapter, we will discuss enhancing your conflict

EXERCISE

Hold out one hand. Make it into a fist, squeeze tight, and keep squeezing. How does this feel? Like freedom? Now release your grip and open slowly . . . feel the difference? This is freedom. Freedom does not come from holding on but comes from releasing. The world tells us we need to win to feel good, but from an emotional standpoint in the midst of conflict freedom comes from changing how we approach the battle. Often we are battling to be heard. Therefore, freedom and release from the grip of frustration can come from when we feel heard.

management skills from the inside out; changing how we think and thinking about how we can change.

The Communication Perspective

We often think of communication as a way of persuading others, of transmitting information, or making our own strong statement. Effective communication is much more than that. Communication creates and shapes meaning. In conflict management, we see that humans construct and manage their differences through communication (Littlejohn & Domenici 2007). Many of us call this approach the "communication perspective" where we privilege communication as the vehicle that creates our social worlds. We "make" our social worlds by our communication choices. One way this perspective can be illuminated in mediations is by asking parties in the mediation, "What kind of world are you making by your communication?" If the parties then describe a negative relationship, we can ask them, "How might you communicate in order to create the relationship you want to live in?" This invites parties into a collaborative conversation where they can discuss how to communicate in order to develop the relationship they want, whether it is a boss and employee, partners in an intimate relationship, or neighbors in a conflict about a barking dog.

Circular Causation and Modeling Behaviors

Circular causation is about cause and effect. Rather than being linear in nature, often conflict can be a continuous cycle of reactions toward one another, which perpetuate the argument. This is particularly common within families, personal and work relationships, or even between neighbors. People who have some on-going relevance to our lives give us opportunities to form cycles of communication.

In mediation when we speak to the parties about making a change in their approach to one another the inevitable response is "I'm always the one who has to change!" All too often we say we desire change in a relationship, but we don't want to be the first to change.

Consider a four way stop with no stop sign. If there is no sign telling drivers to stop, there can be continuous collisions or traffic jams because each person assumes they have the right of way. It's the same with conflict. If no one puts up the stop sign and refuses to *break the cycle* then they will continue to react to one-another in a circular fashion that perpetuates the crazy cycles. If one person stops and deliberately thinks before they react, the cycle can ultimately change. It just may take time and effort.

Consider two siblings, a brother and sister, who frequently argue. The sister walks in the room and her brother says, "Why are you looking at me like that?" That sets off the sister who retorts, "Why are you breathing like that?" Pretty soon an argument ensues over a seemingly innocuous event such as walking in the room. Sounds silly, but consider how many families stop talking for years because of seemingly small conflicts that grew out of proportion.

In these situations, the cause might be something small that grows large because the original conflict was never actually dealt with, rather it was ignored and swept under the carpet. Over time, the origin of the initial conflict is forgotten but the emotions linger. J. L. Moreno, known as the creator of psychodrama, believed that the mind may not remember all of our life experiences, but the body doesn't forget. There is an imprint of emotion in our psyche, even though the original event has been forgotten. In their book *The Arts Go to School*, Booth and Hichiya (2004) quote poet and author Maya Angelo, who said, "At the end of the day people won't remember what you said or did, they will remember how you made them feel" (p. 14). If we can make someone feel different, we could break the negative cycle of conflict.

Have you ever tried to pull out in traffic, but no one stops to let you out? You might become more and more frustrated until finally you see an opening and pull out quickly. You then drive down the road and see someone else trying to pull out. Are you more or less likely to let them out? If you are honest, the answer would probably be no. Since no one helped you, your attitude may be "help yourself." Consider the same scenario, but someone deliberately stopped and let you out in front of them. Later down the road are you more or less likely to let the next person out? The answer is probably yes. That one act of someone letting you out into traffic (or not) can affect your attitude, your day, and how you treat the next person.

In circular causation, people expect us to react in a certain way. Those expectations are what keeps that cycle going because the reactions feel comfortable. However, if we stop reacting in the way they expect and we do something different (and more positive) eventually they will begin to respond differently, more positively than they had before. That's breaking the cycle.

Conflict management and mediation skills are about learning to respond in a new way. In some ways, it's like learning a new language. Reflecting, reframing, summarizing, and acknowledging can seem foreign at first since many of us have not been taught productive conflict management skills, but if you practice these skills in your everyday life using them will eventually become second nature. You will find that you not only get what you want but also what you need. This outcome is vastly different than just winning an argument. The experience of breaking the cycle will enable each party to walk away *feeling* better and have a different outlook on how to handle future conflicts.

In chapter two we discussed the importance of a mediator modeling the behavior they would like to see from the participants. Modeling behaviors works because our brains are hard wired to learn from one another through what scientists call mirror neurons. Mirror neurons in our brains help us learn by mimicking or mirroring others' verbal and nonverbal behaviors. Barry (2009) explains that mirror neurons break down the barrier between us and others "as the actions or expressions of others resonate within us, we empathize and recognize the other as us" (p. 80). Children learn from watching and modeling the behavior of their parents and family members. If you are around little children, you will always know your areas for improvement because they are like little mirrors reflecting our behaviors, and it doesn't stop in childhood. We all emulate someone we look up to and even those we don't. Mehrabian (2017) tells us that in our use of vocal expressions, body language, postures, and gestures, we amplify, restrict, or deny what we say to one another and can speak louder than our words.

It's not enough for the mediator to be aware of the body language of the parties. They need to be aware of themselves as well. In a mediation, if the parties are yelling loudly and the mediator raises their voice to match them, chaos will ensue. Instead, a mediator should lower their voice and speak in a quieter tone. In most cases the participants will ultimately mirror the mediator's tone without even thinking about it. Therefore, leaning in, making eye contact, and smiling are all important nonverbal behaviors that a mediator should use.

The next time you are in conflict, try something different. Rather than yelling, lower your voice. Rather than thinking about your defensive response, really listen and clarify what the other person said to you. "So, what I am hearing you say is that it frustrates you when I borrow your clothes without asking?"

EXERCISE

How something is said can change the whole dynamic of how a person reacts. Read the following vignettes, acknowledge the emotions, and reframe to make the message more positive.

1. Our committee has been meeting every week now for two months. No matter what the proposal or idea expressed, Bob acts like a wet blanket. We only have one more month to complete the plan and implement it: we're running out of time. All he says is, "No, I don't think it is practical," or, "We don't have enough money," or "No, we need more information . . ." We're getting nowhere fast! The rest of us feel like resigning from the committee.
2. You don't understand what it's like to have to sit through a staff meeting like the one we had today! I don't feel like I can be attentive because I am so upset. At times I felt like getting up and leaving.
3. No! that's not what I said. That is not what I want. If no one cares about my opinion and feelings, maybe I should just leave the department. Maybe I'm the oddball here; you all would be happier if I weren't around.

When they say yes, then ask, "What can I do differently?" Putting up the stop sign and making these small changes are not about taking blame, rather they're about stopping the negative cycle and replacing it with positive behavior changes that may save a valued relationship.

Enhancing Skills and Building Capacity

When you begin studying mediation, you should start with basic skills, but good mediation involves so much more. For us, mediation is an art form calling for constant judgment and creative intervention. We have a growing set of tools available to us, but more important are our decisions about *when* and *how* to use those tools. An intervention that would be excellent at one moment in a mediation may be a very wrong thing to do at another moment. A skill that would be perfect in one case may be absolutely inappropriate in another. There is something intangible about competent mediation, something that relies on the sensitivity, sensibility, and wits of the mediator.

Thinking about Goals

A constant question you will face during any case is when and how to use the skills and tools you have developed. When should you restate? Reframe? Set the agenda? Reality test? When is it best to let the disputants argue for a while, and when is it best to intervene? And when you intervene, how should you do it? One way to make these decisions is to think about a set of goals that you may want to accomplish at various points in the mediation. If you think about goals, you ask, "What do I want to accomplish, or what do I hope will happen, at this point in the mediation?"

The Goal Triangle

We like to think of goals as a set of related accomplishments. Figure 5.1 shows a triangle of goals we find useful in making intervention decisions.

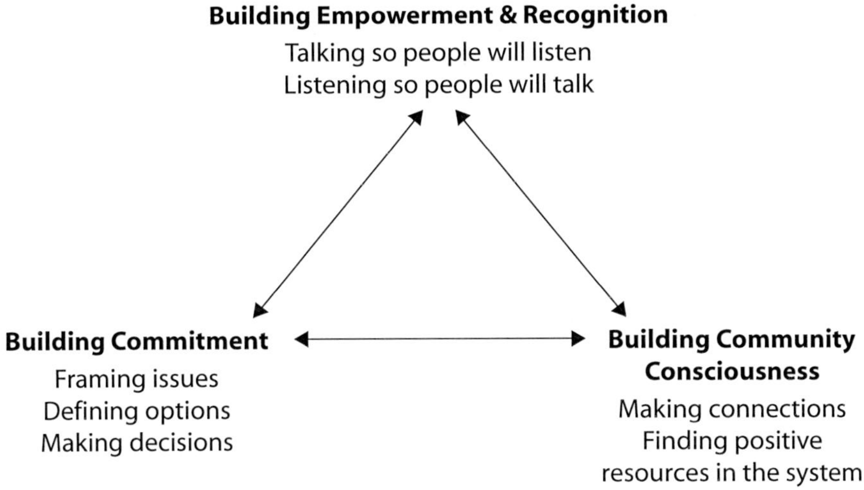

Figure 5.1 Goal Triangle

Notice that these three goals are connected to one another. For example, when the disputants achieve a high level of empowerment and recognition, they create a basis for developing community consciousness and commitment. At any given moment in a mediation, you may feel the need to pay closer attention to one of these goals than to others, but sometimes you may find yourself working on all three at the same time.

Listening

Goal setting skills require active listening. What to listen for is a struggle for many new mediators and students. As we discussed in chapter four, mediators should always have paper and pencil handy to note key things that were said and shouldn't be forgotten (and encourage participants to do the same). One of the first things we want to listen for is common ground between the parties. We also want to listen for values and beliefs that are important to each person, since they are what we may use in a reframe or reflection of feelings. Surprisingly, perhaps most important, is to listen for what someone is repeating.

People repeat what they want heard. When someone repeats themselves in an argument it can be very frustrating. "I heard you!" is often the typical response. As the recipient of that response, we all know how that makes us feel . . . even more angry. Why does it make us angry? We're angry because the other party is not acknowledging what is important to us. They just don't get it. Think about it. As mediators, we understand that once a person has truly "felt" heard on whatever issue is important to them, they will stop repeating themselves. Though it may not seem like a big deal, simply acknowledging what is important to a person can be a pivotal moment in the mediation process.

Acknowledgement Is a Form of Listening

When a mediator acknowledges or uses the reflecting and reframing tools to point out an important issue and the party feels heard they will be ready to move forward. For example: "Jane, I have heard you say a few times now that it upsets you when Sue borrows your shirt without asking. Can you tell me more about that?" If the mediator has hit the right note of acknowledgment, there is a physical change in the person's body language.

First, there might be an actual sigh of relief that someone finally "gets" them followed by nonverbal signs such as uncrossing their arms, leaning in, and making eye contact. This tells the mediator the party is ready to move the mediation forward, may be more receptive to hearing and considering the other party's point of view, and possibly provide more important information about their own perspective.

Think back to Daryl Davis and the exercise in chapter 3 on seeing people as people rather than as problems. Although the participants had fundamental differences in their value systems, they allowed each other the opportunity to speak freely while being listened to actively even when they disagreed. Both Davis, an African American musician and author, and Roger Kelly, the Imperial Wizard of the Maryland Ku Klux Klan, were more receptive to hearing each other's perspective because they themselves first felt heard. Mr. Davis met Mr. Kelly with the objective to listen and to understand. Over time, this openness led to mutual respect that eventually led to a major shift in Mr. Kelly's value system. Active listening is one of a mediator's most powerful tools for change. (See the list of questions and statements that can facilitate movement in the appendix.)

Empowerment and Recognition

Bush and Folger (1994) first wrote about the importance of empowerment and recognition in mediation. *Empowerment* means knowing clearly what is important to you and being able to express this in a way that makes it possible for others to hear it. You have probably seen people from time to time who are very clear on what they want, but the way in which they express it makes others angry, defensive, and unable to take the point seriously. *Recognition* is the ability to see what is important to others—their feelings, their perspectives, their ideas, their interests. Recognition does not mean agreement, but it does mean that you can say, "I see where you are coming from."

Empowerment and recognition are twin goals. They are always tied to one another. You are not truly empowered if others cannot recognize what you are trying to say—and you cannot recognize what is important to others unless they are empowered to express themselves in a way that you can hear.

These twin goals are vital in most mediations, so you will work to help the parties understand their own interests and express what is important to them and do this in a way that makes it possible for each party to at least understand and respect the perspective of the other. Much of what you will do as a mediator—restating, reflecting, reframing, summarizing, etc.—is used at those moments when empowerment and recognition are important.

Community Consciousness

Community consciousness is a feeling of connection between the parties or between the parties and others. When both parties begin to see that they are part of something larger, that they are in it together, that they have common concerns, that they have both contributed to the conflict, and that they have the power to work *together,* they are developing community consciousness. They realize that there is something that exceeds their own individual positions and interests. When the parties see that other people will be affected by their actions, they are developing community consciousness.

A divorcing couple begins to achieve this goal when they start talking about the best interests of their children. A disputing contractor and homeowner accomplish this goal when they see that both want the remodeling project to work. A brother and sister involved in a dispute about what to do with their aging mother accomplish this goal when they come to realize that they are both motivated by a deep concern for their mother's welfare.

You can help parties achieve community consciousness in a variety of ways. For example, acknowledging common ground can help the parties see how they are connected. Pointing out common interests is a way of helping them see the connections between themselves and others. You might even point out connections or ask questions about connections that can help achieve this goal. For example, if a divorcing husband and wife were arguing about what time of the week they should transfer their son from one home to the other, you might ask, "The last time Timmy was sent back to your house, how did he react?" This question could help the parties think about the connection between timing and their son's feelings and behaviors.

Often, too, you can help parties find positive resources to manage their dispute. Even acrimony and argument can be a positive resource, if you use it constructively. A mediator might say, for example, "I see that you both feel very passionately

Student's Journal Entry

Through listening to the stories of both disputants, several shared interests became immediately evident. I imagine this would be so in any conflict—if we gaze intensely enough into the stories.

about this subject. It means a lot to you. What makes this so important in your relationship?" As often happens, the parties may discover that their intense caring is a community asset that can be channeled into a respectable solution.

Commitment

We believe that mediation is ultimately a decision-making process. We want the parties to work together to make conscious, clear, and realistic decisions that work for them. Even the decision not to agree can be a good outcome, especially if it is well considered and right for the disputants at the time.

As a mediator, you will want to give the parties every opportunity to think carefully about what they want to do. Even the decision whether to come to mediation in the first place should be carefully considered. If a party wants to terminate the mediation, that too should be carefully considered and tested. Any process agreement should be tested, and any substantive agreement on the issue should be something that both parties feel is the best thing they can do at the time, perhaps leaving the door open for a different kind of decision later.

In a way, then, a mediation is a series of commitments—not necessarily huge, life-changing ones, but commitments, nonetheless. A small agreement to spend time talking about a certain issue can be an important step forward. A well-tested settlement agreement covering many issues and signed in legal form is another kind of commitment. The parties' decision that they should go to a hearing and let the judge decide is a kind of commitment. So as a mediator, you often find yourself inviting the parties to make careful commitments. Many of the skills you have learned are related to this goal. Issue framing, agenda setting, reality testing, deliberation, and decision making all aim toward this goal.

Living in the Tension

We have worked with colleagues in the Public Dialogue Consortium (PDC) to advance the spirit of dialogic communication, an attitude or approach to communication in which important differences are addressed. Based on the work of Barnett Pearce, the PDC sees dialogic communication as walking a tightrope—balancing in the tension between the differences. In mediation, we see this as remaining in the tension between holding one's own ground while being profoundly open to the other (Littlejohn & Domenici, 2007, pp. 307–308). When parties *hold their own ground,* they share strongly held beliefs but recognize that theirs is one of many perspectives. When parties are *profoundly open to the other,* they do not necessarily agree with the other, but they do show a readiness to listen and to understand the other and to be curious about the good reasons for the other perspective. Mediators can explicitly share this spirit during a break or a difficult moment: "Chris, I see that you shared your strongly held opinion on this issue and at the same time you listened respectfully to Pat's point of view." When parties and mediators are just as concerned about the process of communication as they are about the outcome of the communication process, they may be balancing in the tension.

EXERCISE

Consider a challenging relational issue you have dealt with or are currently experiencing. Write down some aspects of the situation. Who is involved? What type of communication is occurring? How does it feel to be in this interaction? In small groups, discuss these situations and choose one to role-play. Do an informal skit or demonstration of the conflict reflecting the situation at its worst. Then try to perform it again while experiencing the tension of "holding your own ground while being profoundly open to the other." Carefully choose your communication. After the second skit, as a group discuss the communication choices and what was accomplished by this type of communication.

Being Appreciative

Most mediations are pretty negative, at least initially. Yet there is something to appreciate in this negativity. The parties are there, they are willing to talk, and they are sufficiently concerned about their issues that they want some kind of action. We have found in our practice that part of the art of mediation is the ability to explore for the positive.

Parties may be preoccupied with their concerns, problems, and complaints, but if they are to achieve a constructive outcome, that attitude will probably need to shift somewhat. As an artful mediator, you can help.

Behind every concern or problem is a positive shadow. If a disputant is angry because of something the other person did, this disputant must have a better idea of how the other person should have acted. That's a positive vision. We call this the "wisdom in the whining." Every negative statement is motivated by a sense of something better. But when people are upset, they are frequently unable to articulate the "better world" they are imagining. As a mediator, you can help them do this. For example, positive reframing is a way to suggest a constructive way of understanding someone's concern.

As Srivastva and Cooperrider (1999) have written, being appreciative is as much an attitude as a set of skills. It is a way of listening and a way of understanding the conflict. If you can begin to get the disputants to see their differences as a positive resource and to mine their collective assets for solution, they can begin to move toward a constructive future. Here are some of the ways you might invite the disputants to "make the appreciative turn."

- Ask them to tell about a time in which things worked well for them and what made it work well.
- Ask them about their vision for the future.
- Ask them what would be different if their concerns were eliminated.
- Acknowledge and restate positive things they say about one another and about the situation.
- Ask about the resources and assets they have available to "solve the problem."

Co-Mediation

The use of two mediators working together to facilitate the dispute resolution process is common. In community mediation programs, divorce and family mediation, and many court-connected programs, co-mediation has multiple advantages. If cases are particularly complex, it is helpful to have two mediators to untangle the issues. In programs where there are a large number of mediators, particularly when there are apprentice or inexperienced mediators, co-mediation benefits all parties involved. Most mediation programs encourage use of a co-mediator team with similar styles and experiences for conducting mediations. Often the mediators are trained within the program and move up through the ranks as apprentices to another mediator who serves as a mentor. Novice mediators benefit from the experience and from participation with someone who has handled a number of situations. Participants benefit from having one more set of eyes and ears to offer perceptions. The following are advantages of co-mediation:

- The combined communication skills add to the effectiveness of the process.
- Two mediators can better mirror the ethnicity, gender, age, class, and any other considerations a program may be meeting.
- In multi-issue or multi-party cases, the stress can be reduced with two mediators to diffuse tensions.
- The mediators may have substantive expertise that can complement each other (process skills, family matters, legal considerations, empathy, workplace knowledge, etc.).
- Mediator bias is lessened with two mediators, encouraging the greater possibility of trust in at least one of the mediators by disputants.

There are some possible disadvantages to using a co-mediator model:

- For the program, there is an increased complexity of scheduling, increased costs, and the necessity for a greater number of mediators.
- Two mediators can increase the cost for the parties.
- The two mediators may have incompatible styles.

As the mediation field emerges, mediator styles and methods of practice are diverging. Deborah Kolb (1994) explores mediation styles by investigating the different social fields in which mediation occurs. Looking at mediators from arenas such as public policy, divorce, court proceedings, labor grievances, profit making, neighborhood justice centers, and international areas, Kolb notes the diversity in this evolving profession.

The growth of mediation programs in communities, courts, schools, and workplaces has increased the demand for skilled mediators. Inexperienced mediators need opportunities to gain practice. The co-mediator model provides an excellent opportunity, as mentioned above. There is no substitute for participating in actual conflict management. With proper training in communication skills and mediation techniques, novice mediators can continue learning in real-life situations while also contributing to solving problems. Co-mediation is an excellent illustration of the win/win situation we have been describing.

Student's Journal Entry

I realized how hard it is to be a mediator by yourself. Several times I just felt stuck and didn't know what to say next. I think I would need a lot more practice with another mediator.

Chapter Summary

In this chapter, we explored a variety of skills and perspectives that can help individuals and mediators build capacity for better conflict management. A mediator's verbal communication choices are powerful tools, and a mediator's nonverbal communication models positive behaviors for participants to mirror. Finding common ground, empowering, acknowledging, and building community are tangible ways mediators help participants break the negative cycles of conflict and give them new tools to prevent future conflicts. You do not have to be a mediator to learn to break the negative conflict cycles in your life. Remember that effective communication takes deliberate consideration and a lot of practice.

Key Terms

Circular Causation is a continuous cycle of reactions toward one another, which perpetuate argument.

Co-Mediation is the use of two mediators working together to facilitate the dispute resolution process.

Commitment is the decision-making process whereby the parties work together to make conscious, clear, and realistic decisions that work for them.

Empowerment is knowing clearly what is important to you and being able to express it in a way that makes it possible for others to hear it.

The Goal Triangle is a set of related accomplishments a mediator considers when making decisions in a mediation. The triangle's three goals are building empowerment and recognition, building commitment, and building community consciousness.

Mirror Neurons in the brain help us learn by mimicking or mirroring others' verbal and nonverbal behaviors.

Recognition is the ability to see what is important to others—their feelings, their perspectives, their ideas, their interests.

6

Special Concerns

In the last ten years, mediation has established its place alongside our current adversarial systems, the legal system in particular. The emergence of mediation has been called a "muffled explosion" as it tries to work out the kinks that accompany any new societal influence. Scholars in the disciplines of communication, law, sociology, political science, and many others are researching the dilemmas and considerations that accompany this collaborative dispute-resolution process. This chapter will explore four critical issues for the mediation process: appropriateness (intake concerns), the use of a caucus, confidentiality, and ethics. Additionally, this chapter will examine the challenges of dealing with difficult people and mediating large groups in terms of the four critical issues.

Appropriateness

People often express doubts about how well a process like mediation will work and how any of the participants will know if it is successful. People often ask if the win/win approach is too good to be true. It is evident that there are some disputes where a win/lose outcome is the only one available. When there is only one car to be awarded in a divorce agreement, one person will gain possession. When there are two office spaces for three people, one person will get the private space and two will have to share. Most of the time, with mediation, the creativity and good intentions of the participants lead to satisfying outcomes. These outcomes may allow one party to get the car or the private office, but both parties may better understand the other's intentions so both parties do win.

Another question that often arises is whether it is possible for people to change. In attempting mediation, one often hears, "This process looks great to me, but it will be impossible to get my partner to cooperate." If mediators model collaborative communication from their first interaction with parties (whether on the phone or in person), the parties will have a greater chance of adopting these behaviors themselves. Respect and sincerity can inspire similar behavior. Mediators also can encourage parties by showing that the costs of competing are severe, while the benefits of collaborating are rewarding. Mediators can remind the parties that this is their opportunity to create an outcome mutually agreeable to both parties rather than someone else making an unfavorable decision for them, one they might not like. By showing that it is in the parties' best interests to work together, the mediator can help disputants move beyond animosity to a position where cooperation is possible.

Another question often asked is whether the process is too rational for when tensions are high and emotions run deep. Many disputants feel that they are just too emotional or worked up to go through the mediation process successfully. It is important to remember not just to reflect feelings, but to reflect the *intensity* of the feelings. As stated earlier, the emotional part of the conflict often needs an emotion-venting period before the rational, content-related issues can be explored. Mediators can use statements like "You are extremely angry today. Perhaps you should tell us about your anger," "I can see the intensity of your frustration, and we will work today to understand what brought you to this point," or "It must be extremely difficult to consider negotiating when you are so broken-hearted. Let's slow down and learn about your sadness." Our colleague Peter Lang recognizes the importance of working with emotions, seeing them as learned and cultural. An outburst of emotion is a sign of a dream that is not being fulfilled. Mediators can inquire about that dream and identify what needs to happen to realize the dream.

Student's Journal Entry

Because we live in a realistic rather than an idealistic society, there is a need for other forms of conflict resolution besides mediation. This fact is important to remember if one is to practice any of these techniques with living, breathing subjects. Sometimes a fresh approach may work better in a situation where an agreement seems unobtainable. It is the individual responsibility of all professionals who act as conflict resolvers to recognize the point where their efforts are not helping the parties involved.

Collaborative solutions are possible when parties possess the proper attitude and skills. If individuals have a positive motivation concerning the mediation process, they will be more likely to listen to each other and attempt to understand. Parties who do not want to resolve their problems or who are stuck in their positions may not want to use mediation at that time. If it is apparent that the requirement for voluntary participation in mediation is not being met and another form of intervention is needed, referrals can be given to the appropriate agency. Although the decision to mediate usually rests with the parties, mediators and intake workers can assist in that effort. The following questions can help with the decision:

- Is each party at the mediation "table" there voluntarily? Individuals forced into mediation may not be participating in "good faith."
- Can the parties communicate and *hear* each other? Is the emotional component so strong that the parties are unlikely to see past it?
- Are the parties able to identify and express issues and interests for themselves?
- Is each party open to reaching a result that is fair to the other?

When a case is being considered for mediation, there is usually an intake person or intake staff to record some preliminary information, such as general demographics, a short description of the conflict, how long it has been occurring, who are the other parties involved, and who needs to be present to have authority to settle.

When selecting mediators for a case, intake staff must be confident that mediators do not have a conflict of interest with the parties and can hear the issues without bias. Mediators can be biased about issues if they have strong opinions, values, and morals. Mediators may also have some type of affiliation with one or more of the parties. If either of these biases occurs, the mediator has a responsibility to disclose the possible presentiment to the parties or disqualify himself/herself. Highly skilled mediators are able to "turn off" these opinions or biases for the duration of the session.

The intake staff assesses factors such as willingness to use a collaborative process, communication competency, tendencies toward extreme anger or violence, or the necessity of the case being handled by a more appropriate agency (as in the case of a rights or policy violation). If both parties are willing to come to the table and attempt to reach a mutually satisfactory agreement, and characteristics that would hinder the process—such as those discussed above—are not evident, the case should be considered a candidate for the mediation process. Intake workers should not prejudge whether this case will be successful.

EXERCISE

Discuss this situation and the appropriateness for mediation.

Two people married for 25 years request a mediator to help them divorce. One party refuses to seek legal advice, insisting that they can work out a settlement in mediation that satisfies both of them. The other party has sought legal advice and has a firm idea about the type of settlement to reach. They are in their first mediation session and the mediator uncovers this situation. What would you do?

Mediating Large Groups

You may picture mediation as a triad. Something that takes place between two people and a mediator, which is a common scenario in many situations. Mediation is not limited by the size of a group. In fact, there are many situations that require large group participation. This can encompass negotiations in a players strike with Major League Baseball (MLB), conflict between business corporations, school special education mediations with parents, and abuse and neglect mediations within the court system. When possible, the co-mediation model can be very beneficial in situations where there are multiple participants, but with good preparation and a solid plan skilled mediators can effectively mediate these situations on their own.

Rather than dealing with the competing interests between two people, large groups will include a variety of personalities who come to the table with their own sets of positions and interests and each wanting to be heard. These mediations can be particularly challenging as they require a mediator to multitask on a large scale. Paying attention to body language around the table, making sure people are not speaking over one another, addressing difficult behaviors or controlling side conversations happening across the room are all challenges for these types of mediations. Littlejohn and Domenici (2007) discuss the spirit of inclusion within large groups as being more than just bringing people together in the same room. Rather, "It also means designing processes by which different points of view can be heard, respected, and used as a basis for any action that might come out of the discussion" (p. 235).

Large group mediations with which we have much experience occur in the court system. These mediations are focused on children, youth, and families. Most have participants that include parents, each parent's attorney, the attorney for the child (guardian ad litem), the social worker, the social worker supervisor, the attorney for the state, and other professionals. Commonly, mediators ask participants to introduce themselves to all before the session begins. The last several years, we have found it beneficial to have each person introduce themselves *and* tell their goal for the mediation. This may be as simple as a parent stating, "I want to know how to get my kid back" or the social worker stating, "We'd like to develop a strong treatment plan and have the parents work with us." Knowing these stated goals helps the parties recognize common ground right from the start, enabling us to focus on the strengths of our commonalities rather than the weakness of our differences. We can refer back to our common ground when the conversation becomes adversarial.

As in all mediations, the mediator first determines who should be present in the mediation. Unnecessary participants may add chaos to the process. Setting ground rules and goals for the mediation helps maintain order, as the parties determine the most important things to be discussed. Keeping careful notes is an important tool to help the mediator stay organized. These notes can help the mediator redirect conversation back to the task at hand when the parties' focus begins to deviate.

Every mediator has their own style. If a mediator is not comfortable in their role as process manager, they will struggle to maintain control of the process, and the participants often do not respect a mediator who is not confident in their role. This means being able strongly (but politely) to call people out for their behavior (such as side conversations taking place) or to speak up firmly if the conversation gets out of control. However, keep in mind that when a mediator regains control it must be done respectfully and it must maintain *face* for everyone at the table. Mediators use their summarizing, acknowledging, reframing tools, along with references to ground rules with a calm demeanor. Maintaining order and organization is not easy and takes practice. Mediators remain calm and organized by reminding themselves that the outcome of the process belongs to the participants. The mediator's job is to bring an element of peace and calm to the room and guide the conversation. What would your life be like if you could train yourself to use these mediation techniques in everyday life? How might you change your approach to conflict in your family, workplace, or roommate situations?

Managing Difficult Behavior

Throughout this book, we have explored specific mediation tools and how to put them into practice. The key to a successful mediation is being able to communicate effectively with everyone. In mediations, there will be people who challenge and frustrate the mediators and the other parties. Lilley (2006) tells us "There is no such thing as a difficult person, there are just people we need to learn how to deal with" (p. viii).

Have you ever struggled pushing a door to go out only to realize you need to pull to open it? As humans, we are inclined to push back when we encounter a difficult situation, yet we can stop pushing and figure out how to approach the situation in a different way. We will eventually make progress and move ourselves forward. In chapter 4 we discussed active listening. When we listen to understand, it enables us to see where a person is coming from and adjust our reaction appropriately. Some examples of active listening for mediators include adjusting vocal tone to softer instead of louder and posture from closed to open. Still, active listening is even more than that: it is both watching and listening to understand the personality types with whom we are working. Some types of difficult behavior often encountered in mediation are: refusal to participate; domineering personalities; hostility toward other participants; people who interrupt, are loud and emotional, make offensive statements, and/or have side conversations.

Recently, we worked in a mediation where in pre-mediation talks an attorney expressed concern that a certain party was going to dominate the mediation. This statement indicated to the mediators that we possibly needed a stronger opening statement, which emphasized the importance of giving everyone uninterrupted speaking time. While this request may sound simplistic, it is more than just setting down a ground rule. This communication guideline was meant to give the mediator a foundation to refer back to if we did see dominant personalities. The process does belong to the parties, but the mediator is the manager, the guide for that process. The parties look to the mediator as one who will maintain a physically and emotionally safe environment. This takes both strength and finesse.

If we are uncomfortable in dealing with difficult behaviors, then the parties will not respect our position as process manager and chaos could ultimately ensue, causing the mediation to break down. A mediator should maintain a calm presence and use the tools in the mediator toolkit. Rather than play into high emotions, mediators simply acknowledge the emotions, often noting the intensity of the emotion rather than naming the emotion itself. As process managers, it is important to address disruptive behavior directly and politely, to reframe hostile language, and to put a positive spin on it. After a loud emotional argument, summarize concerns and also point out the parties' common ground. For someone who is griping and whining, acknowledge that you see how much they care about the issue but then ask them what solution they think would be helpful. This keeps them constructively focused and moving forward. The most challenging part of being a mediator (or anyone who encounters difficult behavior) is being comfortable dealing with elevated emotions. Think back to chapter 1 and the analogy of the train. If we don't deal with the emotions, the facts won't matter, and the train will eventually derail. (See Managing Difficult Behavior in the appendix for a list of strategies for working with each specific behavior.)

Caucus

The caucus is a break in the mediation process when mediators meet individually with each party. This can be a particularly useful tool when difficult behaviors arise, and the mediator is unable to work through them within the mediation. The break enables the mediator to specifically address issues while also maintaining face for the parties. Information disclosed in a caucus can remain confidential or can be disclosed when the parties reunite, depending on the wishes of the parties in caucus. Remember to ask each party at the end of the caucus session if they would like the content of the caucus to be confidential or if it can be shared with the other party. There are times when a caucus can be helpful and can be considered:

- The mediation has reached an impasse because of rigid positions.
- Mediators suspect there is some hidden agenda or information needed that the parties are unwilling to bring out.
- Emotions are high, and it is evident the parties need a break from each other.
- Issues that are being avoided in a joint session can be clarified in a caucus.
- One or both of the parties seem to need encouragement.
- Mediators have lost control of the session.
- One or both parties would need to take a risk to move further toward agreement.

The use of caucuses varies widely among mediators. Although the benefits can be numerous, there are also some hazards involved. Because of the importance of knowing how to use a caucus successfully and integrating the information gained in the caucus into the full session, inexperienced or not-so-confident mediators may not want to use a caucus. Some disadvantages of a caucus include:

- Time spent with individual parties can appear biased.
- Caucuses dilute one of the strengths of mediation: face-to-face dialogue.
- If there is a request to keep material shared confidential; the material may be necessary for agreement.
- The flow and equilibrium of the session can be disturbed.
- In a co-mediator model, both mediators may not agree on the use of a caucus.

If the mediator decides a caucus session is appropriate, it is important to keep the time balanced and brief. If you are co-mediating, both mediators should be present in the caucus with each party so that both mediators are able to receive the same information, and there is no confusion between the two mediators. If a long time passes, the disputant waiting outside may get suspicious or nervous. The same communication skills used throughout the whole session need to be used in a caucus. Venting of emotions is encouraged, content is re-framed and restated, and acknowledgment of progress should be noted. This separate meeting can produce more flexibility and creativity if used appropriately.

EXERCISE **"Thinking about Caucuses"**

Discuss these situations and what you would do as a mediator:

1. The parties come to a monetary agreement. You see that one party forgot to include a figure from early in the mediation. In caucus, the other party tells you, "Do not tell him about that $50 he forgot."
2. The parties are clearly extremely emotional and have a long history of hurt feelings between them. You feel compelled to separate them and talk to them separately. When you suggest that course of action, one party refuses, saying, "This is the most we have communicated for years." The other longs for a break and says, "I would love to talk with you in private to calm down."

Ethics

Professional organizations for mediators have been developing model ethical codes for mediators for decades. Codes have been developed within organizations, communities, states, and schools. For example, some codes are designed for family mediators concerned with parent-child or domestic issues or for attorney mediators attending to court-connected cases. The Society for Professionals in Dispute Resolution developed *Ethical Standards of Professional Responsibility*. The American Bar Association, American Arbitration Association, and Society for Professionals in Dispute Resolution created *Model Standards of Conduct for Mediators*. These standards are a general framework for the practice of mediation, which may vary from case to case due to laws or contractual agreements.

The mediator's ethical responsibilities include:

Impartiality. A mediator should be free of favoritism or bias in appearance, word, and action. Mediators have a duty to disclose any conflict of interest, which would hinder their neutrality regarding the disputants or the dispute.

Confidentiality. The mediators will inform the parties of the extent to which the content of the mediation will be kept confidential and will maintain that level of confidentiality except in cases of suspected or admitted child abuse or threat of bodily harm to self or others. (See the following section on confidentiality.)

Informed consent. Mediators will ensure that the parties are coming to mediation voluntarily, understanding the process and the mediator's role.

Disclosure of fees. Mediators will ensure that the parties understand the costs and the basis of fees at the outset.

Full opportunity to express interests. Mediators ensure that the parties have opportunity for full expression and will empower the parties to be responsible for their own resolution.

Competence. A mediator shall mediate only when the mediator has the necessary qualifications to satisfy the reasonable expectations of the parties.

Conflict of interest. Mediators shall avoid anything that may create the impression of a possible bias.

Suspension/termination/withdrawal. If participants are unable or unwilling to participate effectively, mediators can terminate the mediation when it is appropriate to do so. Parties should be informed that they also have the right to terminate the process when they feel it is appropriate.

Legal issues. Mediators should not give legal advice. A mediator shall not knowingly participate in an illegal agreement. Lawyers for the parties shall not be excluded if the parties want them present.

Development of the field. Mediators have a responsibility to improve and maintain their professional skills.

These ethical considerations emphasize that mediators have a duty to the parties, to the profession, and to themselves. Because mediation is a profession with ethical responsibilities, it is recommended that those who engage in the practice of mediation follow this code.

EXERCISE **"Ethical Situations"**

Discuss the following situations using the ethical guidelines above:

1. The mediator is on the verge of a settlement in a lengthy and difficult mediation between two coworkers. The mediator has felt that one of the parties looked familiar and finally realized that they used to be neighbors. The mediator is confident that neither party realizes this. What would you do?
2. While escorting two parties into a conference room to begin mediation, the mediator detects a strong odor of alcohol on the breath of one of the disputants. What would you do?
3. In a landlord-tenant mediation, you are in a caucus with the tenant who confides that he slashed his landlord's tires last month out of anger. He asks you not to disclose this fact, even though the mediation is centering on violence in the landlord's parking lot. What would you do?
4. You are in the waiting room with the parties to a mediation. One party calls you aside and whispers that he would like to mediate in the waiting room, because he does not want to limp to the conference room in front of the other party. This is a disability case. What would you do?
5. You have never done any divorce or custody mediations in the past. You are asked to mediate a very informal case where the parties are trying to reach an agreement on visitation for their child. What would you do?

Confidentiality

For decades, mediators have been enjoying a simple, yet powerful component of mediation, the confidentiality of the process. Most mediators say something like this in their introduction: "This mediation process is confidential. Nothing you say in here will go any further than this room. If I take any notes, I will tear them up at the close of this session. If we reach an agreement, you will both get a copy of the agreement, and the agreement will also be filed with this office." Many see that confidentiality is fundamental to the success of mediation and to the satisfaction of the parties. Many interests and concerns expressed in mediation are revealed because of the safety created by confidentiality.

Confidentiality is an important issue, with sometimes conflicting repercussions. Mediation statutes have been implemented, many of which contain privileges shielding the mediator and/or the parties from the disclosure of events that take place in mediation. The American Bar Association Section of Dispute Resolution and the National Conference of Commissioners on Uniform State Laws drafted a uniform mediation privilege that the organizations hope will be adopted by all states for all mediations. Some conversations in our society such as priest/penitent, social worker/client, attorney/client, and doctor/patient are considered privileged. The dilemma with mediation privilege is the creation of a statute that may preclude the traditional legal right to "every person's evidence." Privilege hides evidence for potential legal proceedings and restricts public access to information necessary to our civil society and justice. The hardest advocates against privilege say, "The destruction of notes is obstruction of justice." In fact, a California judge ruled in a 1999 case that a mediator had to testify, despite California's statute that excludes evidence arising in mediations. This ruling found that the benefit of justice outweighed the benefits ensured by mediation confidentiality. One way to avoid the confidentiality dilemma is to tell participants in mediation that you will not voluntarily disclose what you hear.

The debate over confidentiality continues. All alternative-dispute-resolution organizations are watching the proceedings carefully, anxious to see the impact of further legal attention to confidentiality. Some states have certification qualifications for mediators. Some states have qualifications for mediation trainers and hope to see consistent standards for mediation trainings. The voluntary nature of mediation processes has been challenged. Some court programs are now using mandatory mediation, requiring that people use mediation before the next legal step in the process. Watch carefully for the evolution of these issues. The field is evolving and has enthusiastic support. The most idealistic of us find that the mediation mind-set, language, and processes could be the answer to our most pressing social problems.

EXERCISE **"Thinking about Confidentiality"**

Discuss the following situations. What would you do?

1. You are the mediator in a huge environmental case. You know that one party has been convicted in a legal action of a similar pollution violation. You attempted to get the party to acknowledge, in caucus, the previous finding of guilt, but the party refused. What would you do?
2. During a mediation involving two neighbors, it becomes apparent that one of them has been abusing his wife and children. This is not an issue in the mediation. What would you do?
3. One party in your mediation reveals to you in caucus a plan to defraud the other party of money. A hidden bank account, recording devices, spies, and the like are being planned to gain information about the competitor's secrets if a settlement favorable to this party is not reached. What would you do?

Thanks to Anne Thomas, editor of *Making the Tough Calls: Ethical Exercises for Neutral Dispute Resolvers.*

Chapter Summary

The courts, businesses, and attorneys now recognize mediation as a valuable time—and cost—saving form of dispute resolution. The benefits are many. However, it is important to recognize that mediation is not always appropriate; the advisability of mediation should be vetted early. If it is not, the mediator should stop the process and recommend the proper agency or action. Mediators should adhere to ethical standards. Above all, it is important for mediators to recognize their own competencies and to be honest with the disputants if they feel there is a conflict of interest or they are inexperienced in conducting a certain type of mediation. Confidentiality is a significant component in effective mediation and should be honored. Mediators should always be aware of their biases and values—and work from their strengths.

Key Terms

Caucus is a break in the mediation process when mediators meet individually with each disputant.

Collaborative Solutions are possible when parties participate voluntarily, *hear* each other, identify and express their issues, and are open to reaching an agreement fair to both parties.

Competence is mandatory; mediators must have the necessary qualifications to satisfy the reasonable expectations of the parties.

Confidentiality is a significant component in effective mediation and should be honored.

Conflict of Interest exists if mediators show bias toward one of the parties or give that impression.

Development of the Field requires mediators to improve and maintain their professional skills.

Disclosure of Fees requires that mediators ensure parties understand the costs and the basis of fees.

Full Opportunity to Express Interests is necessary to empower the parties to be responsible for their own resolution.

Impartiality is being free of favoritism or bias in appearance, word, and action.

Informed Consent means the parties understand the process, the mediator's role, and participate voluntarily.

Legal Issues are outside the scope of mediation. Mediators should not give legal advice.

Suspension/Termination/Withdrawal is the outcome when participants are unable or unwilling to participate effectively.

7

Completing the Mediator Toolkit

Becoming skilled in mediation or just participating in a mediation session can be life-changing and help develop the social worlds we prefer. This chapter offers final considerations—cultural awareness in mediation, the LARC (listen, acknowledge, respond, commit) method of how to respond to others both in mediation and in life, and the art of mediation through the lens of War and Dance. These add to the mediator's toolkit and strengthen how we respond to conflict in our everyday lives for more positive results. The consideration of cultural differences, the practice of the LARC method, and a commitment to life-long effective communication strengthen the practice of mediation. Managing human difference with collaborative respectful communication gives hope to a world struggling with conflict.

Cultural Considerations

How we define ourselves is shaped by the people with whom we grew up, our families, and our communities. People with whom we share aspects of our life influence the formation of our identity. Multiple similarly influenced people form cultures. Since culture encompasses all the behaviors we have learned—values, customs, morals, language, laws, education, family, communication, and any other capability—it has a profound and often subconscious effect on all interactions. Paul Bohannan (1992, p. 13) refers to culture as "a means of standardizing choices and of sharing successful results of choices made by others in the past."

Cultural differences are varied and not always based on ethnicity. Mediators need to understand that many other group characteristics can surface in mediation. A mediator should be open nonverbally and listen to understand (active listening), creating a safe atmosphere so the parties can appreciate their differences not as barriers to their mediation goals but as potential benefits. Besides ethnic differences, there are age, gender, political, socioeconomic, sexual orientation and preference, workplace experience, background, and religious differences.

Here is just a brief list of some differences you might encounter:

- Some cultures value individuality, while others are more collective or communitarian.
- Some cultures assign more meaning to the context—rituals, relationships, and nonverbal forms. Others give language more credence than context.
- Some cultures are indirect in how they communicate; others want you to say just what you mean.
- Some cultures value silence more than other cultures do.
- Some cultures see eye contact as a way of connecting, but others view it as threatening.
- Some cultures want to communicate directly with others, while other cultures prefer to go through an intermediary.
- Some cultures like to negotiate solutions, while others defer to an elder, wise person, or leader.
- Some cultures are more concerned with tasks—getting the job done—while others are more concerned with nurturing relationships.
- Some cultures like personal acknowledgment; others are embarrassed by it.

Clearly, culture is always an important consideration, but you can never learn everything about all of the cultures you might encounter in a mediation. Even if you were to try to do so, you would run the risk of stereotyping. At a round-table discussion on culture in mediation, someone told us not to look Native Americans in the eye. Immediately, a young Native woman spoke up, "I love eye contact. Please don't avoid looking at me. My grandmother, on the other hand, does not like to be looked at." It is sometimes hard to distinguish between cultural tendencies and personal differences. We think it is a mistake to attribute everything to culture. Culture is one of many factors that make people richly different. In mediation we utilize those differences to help craft agreements that are substantive and enduring.

Sunoo (1990) offers some observations and suggestions that can be helpful when considering conduct for cross-cultural mediation without stereotyping or adapting inappropriately to what you think is a cultural trait.

Expect different expectations—Differing expectations are brought to the bargaining table when individuals from different cultures confront each other. Responses often are misinterpreted, and otherwise assumed "rules of the game" cannot be taken for granted. Some cultures may see elderly persons as wise and deserving of respect, while others may have a different perception, placing 30- to 40-year-old academics at the top of the wisdom scale.

Do not assume that what you say is being understood—The same words spoken in English often have different meanings and emphasis to people from different cultures. In his experience mediating with differing cultures, former president Jimmy Carter (1993) believes it is important to create a framework for discussion by making sure there is shared meaning for words. For example, Carter saw that for one participant in a mediation, to "mediate" was to "dominate"; "compromise" meant "total surrender"; and an "observer" was an "active negotiator."

Listen carefully—Be ready to apply your active listening skills and to reinterpret what you perceive vis-à-vis the cultural orientation of the participants. Determine what concerns and interests each party is trying to communicate with his or her proposal. It takes planning, commitment, and practice to listen actively. This listening includes paying attention to both the verbal and nonverbal communication of the parties. For example, different cultures regard silence in different ways. While one party can indicate agreement by silence (respect for the decision), to another this silence could be seen as indecision or hesitancy. Westerners are often uncomfortable or awkward with silences in conversation or, more specifically, in mediation. They see silence as a negative action, one that signifies lack of interest, boredom, or confusion. Many Asian and Native American cultures see silence as a sign of respect. A talkative person can be seen as a show-off or as an insincere person. Mediators need to be aware of the use of silence, noting the parties' comfort or discomfort and adjusting accordingly.

Seek ways of getting both parties to validate the concerns of the other—For example, a mediator might say, "Margaret, if you were a tailor wanting to promote good faith and recognition of your skilled tailoring, what would you offer to a customer dissatisfied with service?" The mediator then might ask Park to do the same thing concerning Margaret's need for fair compensation for the jacket sleeves that were shortened too much. Role reversals are most effective in sharing perspectives. Always make sure to have both parties participate in the role reversal.

Be patient, be humble, and be willing to learn—Peopleoften expect instant gratification, instant results, and instant responses. Many from other cultures work on a different, often more slowly paced timetable. Impatience is viewed in many cultures as a sign of immaturity rather than enthusiasm; loud displays of confidence may be interpreted as arrogance; and insistence on the rules of the game may be seen as disrespect for how others have learned to interact. In a separate caucus, take time to point out that potential differences could stem from cultural differences, and encourage each party to accept and learn something from the other.

Apply "win/win" negotiating principles to the negotiation rather than traditional adversarial bargaining techniques—Define issues first rather than taking hard initial positions. Discuss interests and concerns of both sides. Try to come up with multiple options for solving the problems of both parties. Apply fair standards to select the options, and work through a consensus process to arrive at solutions rather than using power plays. In the Margaret and Park example, if mediators saw common interests emerge, such as "reputation" or "pride," they could remark, "Let's begin a search for options that could fulfill Margaret's interest in pride in professional clothing and Park's interest in pride in workmanship. Margaret let's start with you. Can you think of an option that could serve the reputation of both of you?"

Dare to do things differently—Throughout the world, there are literally thousands of legitimate and different ways for two parties to reach an agreement. Just because *we* feel comfortable with one set of rules and etiquette does not mean that it is necessarily the most logical, efficient, or desirable method for everyone.

Particular challenges for mediators arise when differences are deeper or less obvious than surface issues and are actually conflicting perceptions of reality. Stephen Littlejohn, J. Shailor, and W. Barnett Pearce (1994) believe that when differences involve incompatible conceptions of morality, justice, and conflict, it is like "one person trying to play chess and another person checkers on the same board" (p. 68). The mediators also come into the situation with their own view of reality, so there are many differences to consider and to coordinate or match if possible.

EXERCISE **"Looking at Culture"**

Do a web search on a controversial topic and list the cultural issues that could or do create conflict. Identify the values that created the differences. Try to discover an underlying interest or goal that could be compatible. Share one or two examples with the class or small group.

To manage these deep differences, Littlejohn et al. (1994) see three paths that may assist in the mediation. The mediators can try to achieve common ground among the various perceptions of reality: (1) the parties can be encouraged to accept the realities of the mediators' process; (2) the mediators can assimilate to the parties'realities—a solution usually not desirable from the standpoint of a mediation program with rules and guidelines that are difficult to bend; and (3) individual attention can be given to each party, helping them to understand issues from the other party's viewpoint.

This option may mean that the mediators reframe issues differently for each party, based on differing perceptions of reality. In other words, mediators must be skilled in basic intercultural communication skills. They may need to step outside of their attempts to discover win/win solutions (collaboration) from time to time and not expect disputants to conform to the mediation process expectations. To suggest this manner of dealing with deep differences in parties' views of reality, Littlejohn et al. find that "the practice of mediation can take on very different meanings as they [mediators] interface with the social realities of various disputants" (p. 82). The challenges created by cultural and other differences add to the responsibility of mediators. The attitudes and skills needed by the mediator are advanced and may take experience to use the intercultural communication effectively.

We find it useful to think of mediation as a "third culture." Almost everyone, no matter what their cultural background might be, will find mediation challenging in some way. There are elements of many cultures in mediation, and each party will need to adjust and adapt their own style and learn new forms of

Words of the Wise

When I am talking with a skillful conversationalist, I am reminded of a master weaver who takes the strands of both my self-concept and his, our relationship, the episode in which we are participating, the speech acts we are performing, and our cultural horizons and braids them into a pattern sufficiently familiar so that I can recognize it and sufficiently unpredictable so that it is interesting.

—W. Barnett Pearce, *Interpersonal Communication: Making Social Worlds*, 1994 (p. 344)

communication in the process. Mediators need to be sensitive to cultural difference, but parties have a responsibility to be flexible also. If you do your job right as a mediator, you will make this transition to a "third culture" as safe and effective as possible.

Conflict in Ordinary Life: The LARC Model

One of the great benefits of mediation is that it can show people new ways to manage their conflicts. This can happen through modeling and practice. Parties notice how you communicate as a mediator, and during the session they can actually practice new forms of communication. These are indirect forms of learning. The model discussed in this section offers one more method and set of skills for personal communication—whether as a mediator, a party experiencing conflict management, or in everyday communication.

EXERCISE **"Practicing LARC"**

Select one of the role plays in the appendix. Find a partner and role play the conflict. One partner should begin by telling his or her side of the issue, while the other listens carefully and asks good questions to clarify and better understand. After a while, the second partner acknowledges the position of the first before stating his or her own side of the issue. Go back and forth several times while listening, acknowledging, and responding. As a last step, make one of the commitments listed in Figure 7.1.

Sometimes, mediators are called upon to teach participants certain communication skills directly in a training session or as part of an orientation to a complex mediation. The LARC (listen, acknowledge, respond, commit) model is a practical and teachable set of skills for conflict management. The model is summarized in Figure 7.1. Notice that LARC consists of many of the basic mediation skills adapted for use in ordinary life.

We think of LARC as a reminder checklist of things people can do when they are faced with conflict. First, they listen.

Then, before responding, they acknowledge the other person's point of view. This is the key to the LARC model—listen and acknowledge BEFORE responding. Figure 7.1 lists several ways in which they might do this. Next, they respond in a constructive way, inviting the other to listen and acknowledge as well. Finally, they end with a commitment. Figure 7.1 lists several kinds of commitment. The important thing is that people in conflict have some sort of concrete next step they are willing to pursue to either settle the matter or to keep the conversation going in a productive direction.

Step 1: Listen

- DELAY judgment.
- ATTEND to as much of the message as possible.
- ASK questions to clarify.

Step 2: Acknowledge

- RESTATE the content of what others say.
- REFLECT the feelings shown by others.
- IDENTIFY interests, goals, values, and needs.
- COMMEND positive contributions.
- REFRAME comments in constructive ways.
- SUMMARIZE what has been achieved.

Step 3: Respond

- STATE your own interests, goals, values, and needs.
- DISCOVER mutual or differing interests, goals, needs.
- FRAME issues and options.
- SUGGEST positive resources for change.
- DISCUSS team implications.

Step 4: Commit

- DECIDE on an appropriate course of action.
- CREATE a positive environment for discussion.
- EXPLORE the problem further.
- SOLVE the problem collaboratively.
- MEDIATE through a third party.

Figure 7.1 The LARC Model

War and Dance

Collaborative models of conflict management are much more than a court alternative. Rather, they offer choices not available in formal adversarial processes, shifting power in a way that gives people an interactive role in managing their problems, an education in forms of communication other than positional bargaining, and a forum for managing difference constructively and respectfully. Whether seen as collaboration (versus adversarial struggle) or cooperation (versus competitiveness), mediation encourages individuals to take an active role in choosing an intervention to help them resolve their dispute. Verderber and Verderber (1992) suggest one indication of the difference:

> When a conflict arises, the variable that first affects the outcome of the conflict is the participant's level of competitive or cooperative behavior. If the participants are competitive, they are likely to introduce negative means in order to "win" the conflict, and as a result, their egos are likely to be involved. Conversely, if the participants are cooperative, they are willing to follow the steps of the problem-solving method: (1) identify the problem, (2) analyze the nature of the problem, (3) suggest possible solutions, and (4) select the solution that best meets the needs determined in the problem analysis. (p. 303)

Littlejohn, Shailor, and Pearce (1994) point out that people enter conflict with differing social realities *moral reality* (what is proper and right, one's basic moral assumptions), *conflict reality* (what conflict means and how it should be handled), and *justice reality* (what is considered just and fair). Lakoff and Johnson (1980) see such orientations as language-based and identifiable by the metaphors used in everyday language. One common metaphor that structures our lives is *argument is war* (p. 4). We see this metaphor almost daily: We win and lose arguments; we attack our opponents; we count our wins and losses (time, money, energy, resources); we strategize and build defenses for our positions. Taking the same metaphor and applying it to conflict, we find that many people in conflict situations seem to live in the metaphorical system in which conflict is war. Lakoff and Johnson (1980) ask us to

> Try to imagine a culture where arguments are not viewed in terms of war, where no one wins or loses, where there is no sense of attacking or defending, gaining or losing ground. Imagine a culture where an argument is viewed as a dance, the participants are seen as performers, and the goal is to perform in a balanced and aesthetically pleasing way. (pp. 4–5)

Perhaps we human beings once enjoyed such a state. Anthropologist Claude Lévi-Strauss suggested that if a Martian were to visit earth, it would conclude that humans had only one truly sustainable successful way of life in their long history—hunting and gathering. This way of life enabled our ancestors to survive against all odds in almost every kind of environment

EXERCISE **"Create a Metaphor"**

Read the following bridge metaphor and then try to create a metaphor of your own concerning conflict, mediation, mediators, or any aspect of the process. You may want to use one of these metaphors and build on it into a story: circle, fan, meal, cart, community, body, game, physics.

> Mediators are like a group of people who build and maintain a bridge over a deep ravine between two villages. The bridge opens avenues of communication between the villages that didn't previously exist. The bridge has to support the weight of any reasonable vehicle driving over it, without denying access to smaller vehicles. It can be used for many purposes—commercial, political, or personal. It can be used as a neutral place to meet as well as a conduit for trade. The maintenance includes ensuring that access is open to both sides and that traffic proceeds in an orderly fashion over the bridge. The builders use guardrails, speed limits, and designated lanes to help ensure the safety of travelers. The builders do all of these things, but they can't force people to use the bridge or to plan their trips across the bridge wisely. They can only hope that they have helped both of the villages to achieve something better in their lives. Their success is not measured by the results of what people do after they have used the bridge, but by the fact that the bridge supported them and provided a way across the ravine.
>
> Jeff Grant

imaginable. The key to its success lay in our ancestors' highly developed ability to cooperate (Ury, 2000).

Perhaps we need a new metaphor. What would be different, for example, if we used the metaphor of *dance* to describe what happens when people are in conflict? What aspects of conflict would become important, what new challenges would we perceive, and how might we re-orient to human differences?

Mediation training is one step toward becoming a mediator, but it is actually much more than this. Only a few of the hundreds of students in our mediation classes have actually become practicing mediators, but our students almost universally report that the class had a major impact on how they communicate in daily life. We think of mediation training as a life skill, not just as a form of professional preparation. Studying mediation can provide tools for improved human relationships in all areas of life. We hope that as a result of this book introducing you to mediation, you begin to think differently about conflict, take a wider perspective on human differences, look in new ways at positions that differ from your own, and interact constructively with others whose lives intersect with yours.

Student's Journal Entry

I remember hearing that mediation could effect change on the whole of a person's life. I thought, "No way. It's a cool thing, but life changing?" My thinking was wrong. I have never been this enthused about anything I've studied, with the exception of learning to read. It has started to effect changes on my life. My temper doesn't show itself anywhere near as much as it used to. I see more opportunities than I ever had before in my personal life, in school, in my future. Some of these opportunities have appeared in the middle of situations I would have previously seen as nothing more than a depressing drag. I've only begun to scratch the surface of where I think that ADR will take me.

Chapter Summary

Mediators need to consider cultural differences, keeping in mind that individual differences may outweigh cultural inclinations. The LARC Model skills of listen, acknowledge, respond, commit are teachable to all participants. The metaphors we use shape how we view conflict. Students who study mediation almost universally report the experience has had a major impact on how they communicate in daily life.

Key Terms

Collaborative models of conflict management offer choices not available in the formal adversarial processes of the court system. They shift power in a way that gives people an interactive role in managing their problems.

Conflict Reality is what conflict means and how it should be handled.

Cultural Differences are varied and not always based on ethnicity. They may include age, gender, political, socioeconomic, sexual orientation and preference, workplace experience, background, and religious differences.

Culture encompasses all the behaviors we have learned, which include values, customs, morals, language, laws, education, family, and communication.

Justice Reality relates to what is considered just and fair.

The LARC Model of listen, acknowledge, respond, commit is a teachable set of skills for conflict management.

Moral Reality covers what is proper and right, one's basic moral assumptions.

Appendix

AGREEMENT TO MEDIATE

1. Mediation is a process which creates an opportunity for all Participants to discuss their concerns. The Participants choose what they will talk about in mediation and how best to work together in the future. An agreement reached should be done so freely and voluntarily.
2. The job of the mediator is to conduct and guide the mediation process. Mediators have the right to exclude persons whose behavior undermines the integrity of a fair mediation process.
3. Participants must agree who will be involved in the mediation process and in doing so, agree to remain courteous and respect the opinions of others. The parties that are participating in mediation must have authority to settle and resolve issues.
4. Our mediators are trained and skilled to promote constructive communication and problem solving. They do not provide legal services or advice, nor do they impose any resolution on the Participants. It is the not the role of the mediator to express who is right or wrong, rather the mediator will help the Participants work toward an agreement acceptable to one another.

5. The Mediation Procedures Act protects the confidentiality of all mediation communications. Chapter 11 NMSA (2007 Supp). The Participants agree not to talk later about what was said in the privacy of mediation. Except as otherwise provided in the Mediation Procedures Act, or by applicable judicial court rules, all mediation communications are confidential, and not subject to disclosure and shall not be used as evidence in any proceeding.
6. Any agreement reached through mediation must be mutually acceptable and signed by each Participant. A written record of the mediation signed by all Participants is not confidential and is binding and enforceable. The Participants take their written record with them after the mediation.

My signature below indicates that I have carefully read, and understand, this agreement, and I will comply with the terms of this Agreement to Mediate.

________________________	________________________
Participant Signature/Date	Participant Signature/Date
________________________	________________________
Participant Signature/Date	Participant Signature/Date

Sample Mediation Introduction

Hello! Welcome to mediation at the Community Mediation Center. My name is Heidi Ricci, and this is Kathy Isaacson. We will be your mediators tonight and would like to take this opportunity to commend you on choosing this method to address your dispute. Would a first-name basis be OK tonight? Thanks Jim, Jane. Let's begin by defining the mediation process and letting you know what you can expect here tonight.

Mediation is a conflict management process where mediators are impartial third parties who help you work out an understanding that is acceptable to both of you. We will help you explore the situation. We will begin by asking you both to explain the situation that has brought you here tonight. We want to help create a comfortable and productive session in which you can explore your issues and generate options. Our goal is to help you achieve an outcome with which you are both comfortable.

Our role here tonight as mediators is to serve as facilitators. We will not make decisions for you or give suggestions. We are not here as lawyers or judges or counselors, but as communication guides to discuss solutions for the future.

Anything you say here tonight will be confidential. You may see us taking notes and you are free to do so, too. These notes will be destroyed at the end of the session.

We follow some common courtesy guidelines. It is in everyone's best interests to keep our discussions civil and balanced. Everyone will have a chance to speak. Do either of you have any guidelines you feel would be helpful?

Because we encourage good communication, we prefer to work in a common session, but sometimes we find it necessary to call a caucus—a break in the process—where we will meet with each of you separately. Information given in a caucus may be kept confidential if you so desire.

Do either of you have any questions? How would you like to begin?

Questions and Statements That Can Facilitate Movement

The following phrases help individuals offer information on content and feelings. These statements can be used in the storytelling stage, problem-solving stage, or agreement stage to clarify issues, to elicit more information, and to check possible options or solutions to make sure they will provide a workable solution.

Let me see if I've heard you correctly; you're saying . . .

It sounds to me like you feel . . .

Can you tell us some more about . . .

What happened to lead up to this situation?

Are there any other details that contributed to this problem?

What do you need to feel better about this situation?

What could ____ do to help this problem be resolved?

What is it about _____ that makes you feel ______?

Can you explain to us what you just heard _____ say?

What will this mean to you?

How will this affect your family/working relationship?

I hear you saying . . . is that correct?

So you wish that . . .

The following questions are "generative" in that they generate insights and move the process forward.

What's emerging that is new for you? What new connections are you making?

What have you heard that has real meaning for you? What surprised you? What puzzled or challenged you?

What is missing from the picture so far? What are we not seeing? Where do we need more clarity?

If there is one thing that has not been said but is needed in order to reach a deeper level of understanding/clarity, what would that be?

If our success were completely guaranteed, what bold steps might we choose?

How can we support each other in taking the next steps? What unique contribution can we each make?

Statements That Can Stop Movement

Some phrases can hinder individuals from exploring issues, revealing content and acknowledging feelings. These statements imply judgments or advice on the mediator's part that takes control away from the parties. These types of statements also can reduce trust in the process, as the parties feel the control being taken away from them. Certain statements evoke defensiveness, as parties feel like they have to justify their actions and statements.

You ought to/you need to . . .

Why didn't you do . . .?

That doesn't seem like a very important issue. I suggest that you . . .

That would be a bad choice for you. You are wrong about that.

How could you feel that way—you know better than that!

Everyone has those feelings.

You can do better than that.

Don't feel like that.

Don't believe that way.

Let me give you my analysis of this situation.

Managing Difficult Behavior

Here are some strategies for helping to transform negative behavior into a more positive pattern:

Interruptions. Acknowledge the person's need to talk.

"I can see you have strong feelings on this, Bob, and we'll get to you in just a moment. In the meantime, I want to hear the rest of Jane's comment."

Non-participation. Acknowledge listening and invite comment.

"Jim, I see you have been listening for a while, and I wonder what you are thinking about all of this."

Disruptive behavior. Address it as a group problem.

"I notice we've been sidetracked a number of times. I wonder how we can make sure our discussion stays focused."

Side Conversations. Talk to the offending individuals privately.

"Betty, I've been distracted by your whispering in the back row. I'm sure it's nothing, but I just wanted to check with you to see if there is something I should know."

Offensive statements. Let the group handle them.

A group member makes a racial slur. Pause for a moment to let it sink in. See if anyone comments, then move on. If the problem persists, ask the group if they would like a ground rule on respectful language.

Hostility toward others. Reframe it and remind the group of the ground rules.

Upon hearing one participant call another a thief remind everyone about the ground rule of maintaining respectful language. "We have to work together, so let's make it as easy as possible."

Loud, emotional argument. Interrupt, acknowledge, summarize, and take a break.

"Just a minute, just a minute. Excuse me. I can see that Tom is very upset about Elizabeth's new accounting system, and Elizabeth you don't appreciate Tom's argument about it. I can see that both of you care about how records are kept, and I want to suggest that we look at that issue calmly. Let's take a break and get back to this situation when we return."

Griping and whining. Acknowledge the caring, state the positive vision behind the person's complaint, and ask for a solution.

"I see you really care about making improvements. I appreciate your vision for an effective working environment, and I'm wondering what ideas you have for improving the situation."

Role Playing

Role playing is an essential part of mediation training and skill development. It will give you an opportunity to practice mediation skills in a safe environment in which you can learn from your successes and mistakes. In a typical role-playing situation, you will take the role of mediator, party, or observer. In many mediation trainings, coaches are solicited for the role-playing experience. These coaches are often experienced mediators from the community who volunteer to assist with the coaching of role play experiences.

In order for role playing to work, the players must make the situation as realistic as possible. You will be a member of a small group seriously developing important life skills, so avoid giggling, mentally escaping, loafing, or generally trying to get out of working productively. If you do not take the role play seriously, you hurt your own as well as all of the other participants' learning experience.

When you play the role of mediator, you may not know anything about the situation or the case in advance. This will give you a chance to practice good active listening skills during the storytelling phase as you uncover the issues as well as the parties' interests. Before the mediation begins, the mediators should plan how to arrange and utilize the space. (How should the chairs be set up? Where should the mediators sit? Should you use a white board or flip chart to record notes?) Mediators should also discuss how to present the introduction and how to divide the segments of the introduction. You should give the disputants a copy of the Agreement to Mediate to read while you are planning and arranging. Be sure to have them sign it during the introduction. Do not rush the mediation process. Allow plenty of time to explore the issues and to reach an agreement, but do not force an agreement. If the parties do reach agreement, use the Mediation Agreement form provided in the appendix and practice your agreement writing skills. You may achieve any of the following outcomes by the end of the session:

- Draft an agreement
- End the mediation without an agreement
- Schedule an appointment for another session (which would not actually be held)

Being a party is a valuable part of role playing. Here you will get an idea of what it feels like to be involved in mediation. As a party, you should study your role carefully. If separate role sheets are provided for the two parties, do not read the other person's role, and please do not meet ahead of time to discuss or orchestrate the role play with the other person. You can use notes or refer to the role sheet during the role play if you wish. Parties should "get in role" and improvise as necessary during the role play. When you improvise, be realistic. You can make up details not on the role sheet, but don't make up things that contradict the role. Avoid making up details just for the shock value. There is a difference between reasonable improvising and wholesale fictionalizing. Try to get into the part emotionally as well as factually. Ignore the names given to disputants and use your own name instead, and make any necessary gender adjustments. (For example, if the role assignment says you are a brother, but you are a woman, turn the role into that of sister.) Avoid telling the whole story all at once. Let out information gradually as real people do.

As a role-play party experiencing conflict, you have a tricky job to do: You must stay in character but be fair to your classmates who are playing the mediator role. In other words, be realistic, but don't be so difficult that the mediator will not be able to get a good mediation role-play experience. As a general strategy, you might be somewhat selfish and competitive at first and move gradually toward collaboration as the mediation progresses.

When you take the part of observer, you will be less active. But observing is no less important than the other roles. You should listen carefully, imagine yourself as mediator and think about what you would do, make note of the successes of the mediators, and consider ways in which the mediation might have been more successful. You are encouraged to take notes. If there is time, the coach or the instructor will allow you to share your perceptions. As observer you may have to step in for a classmate who does not show up as scheduled. Be prepared to take the part of a mediator or party if necessary.

Coaching can be a vital part of the role-play experience. In coached role plays, the coach will have time to provide feedback at the end of the session. The coach can be helpful in other ways too. If you get stuck, you might turn to the coach for help. Some coaches prefer to interrupt the play to provide feedback at the moment when something interesting happens. If you would prefer not to be interrupted, please let your coach know this ahead of time. Feel free to ask your coach questions. You might want to replay situations after getting the coach's feedback. (See Guidelines for Mediation Coaching later in this appendix.)

Cases for Role Playing

Note: These cases are adapted from scenarios created by our students over the years. We wish to thank these students and others for their continued contribution to the materials and concepts we include in our trainings. The first few cases are simple and can help integrate skills and methods used throughout the book. The latter cases are more complex and are suitable for the end of the training or course. ***Please do not read through these cases in advance as you will be assigned a role when the role play exercises begin.***

One Roommate Too Many

Alex and Sam are roommates for the second semester in a row. The fall semester went well, however Sam started dating Jo over winter break. Ever since the next semester started Jo has been practically living in the college apartment with Alex and Sam. Jo eats Alex's food and doesn't replace it. Sam and Jo make a mess in the kitchen and rarely clean up after themselves, even though Sam promises to "take care of the mess." It is often several days before Sam does clean, which really irritates Alex. Lately, whenever Alex comes home from work or classes, Sam and Jo are in the living room watching the one television in the apartment, which was provided by Alex. Midterm exams are approaching and Alex is becoming very frustrated trying to study with Jo constantly in the apartment. The last straw for Alex is that Sam and Alex pay for the two parking spots that come with the apartment and lately Jo parks regularly in Alex's spot. Not one for conflict, Alex seeks out the campus mediation program to see if they can resolve this situation before there's a big blowup.

Workplace Conflict

This is a case between the owner of a private advertising agency and the supervisor of the other five employees of the agency. There has been some underlying tension in the workplace—a small building with one main common area, an office for the owner, an office for the supervisor, and five cubicles for the artists. In the common area is a conference table, copy machine, fax machine, coffee and snack area, and reception area.

The owner has built this business from scratch. In the increasingly competitive advertising community, this company has struggled to remain one of the top three advertising agencies in Albuquerque for the last ten years, but hopes to expand with a branch office.

The owner has an authoritarian style of doing business, desiring efficiency without sacrificing quality. This owner handselected the supervisor and the five artists, leads the weekly staff meeting, sets the agenda and issues, and makes decisions. The banner over the owner's desk reads, "The man who rows the boat doesn't have time to rock it." The message coming from the owner is to keep the momentum but not to sacrifice any employees.

The supervisor doesn't feel valued or respected. Managing five professional artists and keeping them motivated and satisfied is an immense responsibility. The supervisor feels continually shut out at staff meetings. The supervisor wants to offer professional education and incentives such as going to conferences and workshops and trying new techniques. The supervisor feels that the success of major advertisers is the result of flexibility, the opportunity to "stretch." Three of the artists have a special interest in a new video technique using 3-D images, and the supervisor is interested in encouraging experimentation with a couple of the clients.

The simmering conflict between the supervisor and the owner boiled over during the last staff meeting. The supervisor was incensed after the owner took credit for a slogan advertising a new juice drink. The supervisor remembers mentioning the idea for the slogan to the owner in a conversation that week. At the staff meeting, the owner presented it as their own individual brainstorm. This led to a short, heated exchange of words at the meeting. Before they both left the office that day, they had words again and tempers rose further. The supervisor said the issue is much bigger than just credit for that one idea; it is a matter of respect where respect is due. The owner sticks to the issue of the credited idea, remembering clearly when it was hatched. The supervisor suggested mediators from the local neighborhood association to help them resolve the conflict. The owner agreed, not wanting to waste time arguing and affecting productivity.

Home for the Holidays

A college couple has been dating for eight months. Thanksgiving and Christmas are approaching. Both of their families live within an hour of the university. Avery's parents are divorced. The mother has a much younger boyfriend and is very laid back. This mother has always cooked Thanksgiving dinner at her house. The father remarried and his new wife doesn't cook, but she likes to go to her family's home for dinner late in the day. Kennedy's parents are married and very traditional. They believe the holidays are important and the entire family should be together. Their Thanksgiving dinner is served at 1:00 PM sharp. For the college couple, this holiday season is significant since it will be their first together and their relationship is becoming serious. They want to meet each other's family. It is three weeks until Thanksgiving and the couple has been arguing frequently about how to handle this situation. All of the parents have been inquiring and inviting them to holiday gatherings. The couple decided to seek help from the campus mediation program.

Barking Dog

A local resident has been complaining about the barking of the neighbor's dog. (S)he attempted to bring the matter up with the neighbor but has never been able to find this person at home during the day. (S)he contacted the Neighborhood Dispute Resolution office, which then called the neighbor and issued an invitation to mediation.

The complainant, a twenty-year resident of the neighborhood, has been increasingly bothered by the barking of the dog at night, particularly about 3 AM. (S)he and his (her) spouse are both retired and have trouble getting back to sleep once awakened. They are proud of their neighborhood activities and are active in the local association. Each year, they host the neighborhood picnic. They occasionally have their grandchildren over for the night, which is particularly troublesome when they are awakened. This disputant feels very generous in not calling the police and using mediation instead.

The dog owner is a pilot with Fasttrack Airlines. (S)he works odd hours, sleeps odd hours, and is a single person who moved into the neighborhood six months ago. Having a dog is an important security precaution since (s)he came from a large city where there was a lot of crime. This resident has never before had complaints and thought the dog would be an asset to the neighborhood. (S)he hopes to stay in the area for a long time and has just been too busy to meet the neighbors. A stubborn person, (s)he is a firm believer in personal rights, especially in one's own yard and home. The invitation to mediation was a surprise and an imposition on his (her) busy schedule.

Tenant-Landlord

Tenant rents a small bungalow in the far back end of Landlord's property. The parties have a verbal agreement that Tenant would rent for another year, but neither party is happy with the way things are going. Tenant pays $600 a month and was hoping to have a washer/dryer installed, as was discussed in a conversation six months ago. Landlord wants Tenant to share more in the yard responsibility and wants to increase the rent by $25 a month.

Tenant wants to continue to rent the apartment but is a student and cannot afford any additional cost. Tenant had believed that Landlord "promised" to put in the washer/dryer and thinks Landlord is putting that off so the rent can be raised. Tenant wants to continue to pay the $600 a month for the next year and is then willing to renegotiate the rent. Tenant wonders why Landlord is now going back on promises. Tenant enjoys the company of Landlord, and they previously would talk and share a cup of coffee.

Landlord wants to maximize potential profit from rental property. Similar rentals in the area go for at least $700 a month, and Landlord feels that this has been quite a generous arrangement. Landlord was recently divorced and is short of funds. Putting in a washer/dryer is an impossibility unless the rent could be raised. Landlord is also hesitant to give anything more to Tenant, since Landlord has been expecting some help with the yard work and is not seeing any. Landlord feels overwhelmed with responsibility and sees that raising the rent to an appropriate amount and sharing some of the responsibilities could put them both on the right path.

A Family Dispute

Role One:

Please do not read the other player's role.

Several years ago, your parents got divorced after 36 years of marriage. After the divorce, your mother had a nervous breakdown and was hospitalized for 10 months. The hospital was in your hometown, where your parents had lived and where your sibling still resides. You live about 140 miles away.

Because your brother (sister) lived close by, you agreed that (s)he should have your mother's power of attorney over her financial affairs. This was a considerable responsibility because of the divorce settlement. Your mother received a $50,000 cash settlement, half of the furnishings in the house, and $1,400 monthly alimony for life. While your mother was in the hospital, you and your sibling agreed that the $50,000 would be safer in your sibling's name because you were afraid the hospital would seize the money. Your brother (sister) agreed that this money would only be used in case of emergency. The two of you further agreed that when your mother got out of the hospital, she would live with your sibling and that the cash would remain in your sibling's name. Since there was no room for your mother's furniture, you agreed to store it in your garage.

Everything seemed to be going well for the first few years. Your mother improved, but because of advancing age and memory loss was unable to assume responsibility for her own affairs. You visited your mother whenever possible, which would give your sibling and his (her) spouse a chance to have time to themselves.

Now things have changed. Your brother (sister) ended up having an affair, which resulted in divorce. Because of this crisis, your mother had to come and live with you. The first thing you did when your mother moved in was check her financial situation, and you were shocked. You found that her taxes had not been filed for years, her medical bill payments were months overdue, and her credit cards were all over their limits. You also discovered that her savings account, once $50,000, was reduced to half that amount. You confronted your sibling about this, and s(he) told you that after the divorce s(he) needed a car and used $25,000 as a loan. (S)he said that (s)he planned to pay it back.

Your mother has been living with you now for 7 years, and you have been able to correct all of her financial problems. You did this by selling your mother's furniture and applying some of the proceeds as a down payment on a larger home with an extra bedroom for your mother. This living arrangement seems to be working out nicely.

However, you are still very concerned about the savings account, which remains in your brother's (sister's) name. You have no idea how much money is left. You have tried to broach the subject with your sibling, but (s)he always changes the subject and is never willing to talk about it directly. An attorney friend of yours advised you to try mediation, and your sibling agreed.

Role Two:
Please do not read the other player's role.

Several years ago, your parents got divorced after 36 years of marriage. After the divorce, your mother had a nervous breakdown and was hospitalized for 10 months. The hospital was in your hometown, where your parents had lived and where you still reside. Your sibling lives about 140 miles away.

Because you lived close by, you agreed that you would take your mother's power of attorney over her financial affairs. This was an onerous responsibility because of the divorce settlement. Your mother received a $50,000 cash settlement, half of the furnishings in the house, and $1,400 monthly alimony for life. While your mother was in the hospital, you and your sibling agreed that the $50,000 would be safer in your name because you were afraid the hospital would seize the money. The two of you agreed that this money would be used only to meet serious needs. The two of you further agreed that when your mother got out of the hospital, she would live with you and that the cash would remain in your name. Since there was no room for your mother's furniture, your sister (brother) agreed to store it in her (his) garage.

Everything went pretty well for the first few years. Your mother improved, but because of advancing age and memory loss was unable to assume responsibility for her own affairs. You found that you had to take more and more care of her, which put a lot of stress on your marriage. Just having another person in the house was difficult. Still you felt a personal responsibility and did your best. You spent many sleepless nights and long days giving your mother the support and care she needed. You asked your sister (brother) to help, but all (s)he would ever do was visit for an occasional weekend.

Your spouse spent more and more time away from home, leaving you with the sole responsibility of caring for your mother. During this period a family friend showed a lot of concern for you and provided the emotional support you needed. You began to spend more time with this person and ended up falling in love. You realized that your marriage was on the rocks, and the best thing would be a divorce. This was an extremely hard time for you. For one thing, you were short on money and had to borrow from your mother. You did use her credit cards on occasion, but you kept track and plan to pay back this money as soon as you can.

After your divorce, you did not have a car, and you had no way to provide transportation for your mother. This was fairly serious because you needed to get her to the doctor, take her for rides, etc. You felt that this was what the savings account was for, so you decided to use some of the money to buy a reliable car. You spent $25,000 for this purpose. During this period, your sibling seemed very concerned about your mother's welfare, so you agreed to have her go live with your sibling for a while.

This change seemed to be good for your mother, so it has become permanent. The only thing that bothers you is that (s)he sold your mother's furniture to provide a down payment on a new house. You have been very angry about this, but your precarious personal situation has demanded all of your energy, so you have not been able to confront her (him) about it. Your relationship has become tense because of this and because your sibling keeps pestering you about the savings account. Things finally came to a head recently, when (s)he suggested that you go to mediation. You welcomed the chance because it would allow you to clear the air.

A Work Conflict

Role One:

Please do not read the other player's role.

You are the Facilities Manager for a university athletic department. You have considerable responsibilities and normally have an assistant to help. Unfortunately, your assistant recently got another job, and you have been overwhelmed with the heavy workload. Your boss, the Athletic Director, has told you that funding is not available to fill your assistant's position and you will have to go it alone for a while. In desperation, you appealed to him for help. Specifically, you asked if someone could take over the special events contracts, one of your heavy responsibilities. Your boss was sympathetic and said he would try to find someone to take over that responsibility.

Within a few days, he reported back to you that the Ticket Manager would take over special event contracts, but all final decisions and scheduling of special events must be approved by you. You were not altogether pleased with this decision because you have found this person to be somewhat uncooperative in the past. For some reason, you feel that the Ticket Manager does not take you seriously. You are also concerned because the Ticket Manager is your equal in the organization chart and also reports to the director.

As time went by, your fears were realized. Your contracts "assistant" has made several decisions and closed contracts without your approval. Usually, you have found out about these decisions after they were made. You have become extremely frustrated about this. A couple of weeks ago, you tried to talk to the individual, but the conversation turned into an argument and nothing got resolved.

To make matters worse, after this terrible meeting you got a call from a coworker who was also upset with this person. In this telephone conversation, you vented your bad feelings about your new assistant. Suddenly, the temporary contracts manager, who had been listening on the line, angrily asked what was going on. This led to an angry exchange on the phone.

The past week has been hell. Your conflict has created a lot of tension throughout the workplace, and the Athletic Director has told both of you to figure out how to solve the problem. To your surprise, you received a call from the Mediation Center saying that your colleague wanted to have a mediation with you, and you have nervously agreed.

Role Two:

Please do not read the other player's role.

You are the Ticket Manager for the athletic department at a large university. This is a major responsibility, and you have a small staff of three to help. You and your staff are normally quite busy, but you pride yourself on your ability to make decisions quickly, organize things, and get the job done.

One afternoon your boss, the Athletic Director, asked if you would be willing to take on the responsibility of negotiating special contracts. This is normally the responsibility of the Facilities Manager, but this person's only assistant recently left, and (s)he needs help in this area for a while. You were a little concerned because the Facilities Manager is your equal in the organization chart and also reports to the Athletic Director. You also were somewhat worried about taking on such a major function from another department. You do not know the Facilities Manager very well, but you have found this person to be a little shy and withdrawn, somewhat hard to work with. Still, you figured that with your organizational abilities, you could manage the new assignment, and agreed. Besides, you really would not need to coordinate much with the Facilities Manager on these contracts as long as you kept him (her) informed.

Actually, the job went well. You integrated it into your other responsibilities easily and proudly negotiated several high-paying special events. You were really not aware of any difficulty until the Facilities Manager confronted you a couple weeks ago. (S)he said that (s)he was supposed to approve everything in advance and was angry that you had left her (him) out of the loop. The idea that you would need her (his) prior approval on contracts is unacceptable to you. You would not be able to do the job, along with your other responsibilities, if you had to do this.

Things got worse a few days later when you picked up the phone to make a call. You found a key that was not lit, hit it to call out, but discovered that someone was already having a conversation on this line. You would normally have hung up immediately, but you heard your name spoken, and it turned out that it was the Facilities Manager telling someone else how terrible you were. You were shocked and immediately asked what was going on. There was a pause, and the other party hung up. The Facilities Manager, however, stayed on the line and read you the riot act. In all your career, you have never been so insulted.

The past week has been hell. Your conflict has created a lot of tension throughout the workplace, and the Athletic Director has told both of you to figure out how to solve the problem. You decided to try mediation and called the Mediation Center. They told you that they would contact the other party and get back to you. To your surprise, they reported back that (s)he would be willing to mediate, and a date was set.

The Conference Room

Role One:

Please do not read the other player's role.

You are a senior staff member in the education department of your company and responsible for the corporate management training program. You develop new courses continuously and offer them as needed. This training is mandatory for all new managers and must be completed within a year of being appointed to a management position. As new courses are offered, all managers are strongly encouraged to enroll as soon as possible. In addition to the management training, you are often asked to conduct team-building workshops for individual departments dealing with various communication issues, including diversity and assertiveness. With all of this, you stay quite busy.

When the dates of a training are established, your final step is to reserve the space. You always use the corporate conference room, a very nice, well appointed room. It is perfect for your training, participants love it, and you have all the equipment already installed in the room.

At present, however, you are very upset. You told the education department administrative assistant to reserve the corporate conference room for your latest round of trainings, which were scheduled two weeks hence. (S)he said that the room had already been reserved by another trainer, Joe Smitter, who had been recently employed in the education department. You really do not know Joe very well, but you believe that because of your seniority and the fact that you always use this room, you should be able to have first choice. You asked the administrative assistant to inform the new trainer that he will have to find another space, and (s)he refused. You complained to your boss, the Director of Education, who referred you to mediation.

Role Two:

Please do not read the other player's role.

You are the administrative assistant in the education department of your company. This department is responsible for developing and offering training courses for employees. One of your many jobs is to schedule rooms for the various trainings. The procedure is that a trainer will request a room, and you will put it on the schedule. Often trainers request particular rooms that they like. If the desired room is available, you schedule it, on a first-come, first-served basis. If the room is not available, you schedule a different one. This system works well, and you have been complimented many times on the fairness and efficiency of your room scheduling system.

One of the most popular rooms is the corporate conference room, which is quite beautiful and fully equipped. Many trainers in your department prefer this room, and it is often hard to get. Because of conflicts with this room and other rooms, you have asked everyone to be sure to get their room requests to you no later than one month before the scheduled training.

Right now, though, you are very upset. One of the senior staff members put in a request for the corporate conference room two weeks prior to his (her) scheduled training, and it was already reserved by Joe Smitter, a recently hired trainer. When you told the senior staff member that the room was not available, (s)he became very upset and told you to reschedule Mr. Smitter's training in another room. This would be a clear violation of your first-come, first-served policy, so you refused. The senior staff member stomped out of your office.

Soon after this, your boss, the Director of Education, told you that the senior staff member had complained and the two of you should work out the problem in mediation, so here you are.

The Dog Bite

Role One:

Please do not read the other player's role.

You, your spouse, and your 12-year-old son Tim have lived for 11 years in a nice section in the North Valley. The other member of your family is Benji, a four-year-old beagle. Your home lies on a large, quarter-acre lot, which is beautifully landscaped with a pretty fenced back yard. The back yard has a nicely kept 2–3 foot flower bed along the fence. The fence itself is 5 feet tall, constructed of 6 inch wire mesh fastened to wood posts.

Your family is doing quite well. You are happy and earn a high income of $180,000 per year. This is considerably higher than the average five-digit family income of the neighborhood. You do not flaunt your money and consider yourself to be a good neighbor.

Something bad has happened, however. A couple of weeks ago, your doorbell rang on a Saturday evening. Benji heard it also and was barking at the top of his lungs. You opened the door to find your neighbor and his (her) 12-year-old son Mark. Although you do not know this family very well personally, Tim and Mark have been playmates off and on for several years. Mark's family lives next door, and their back yard is adjacent to yours, separated by the fence.

After you opened the door, you immediately saw that Mark's arm was bandaged and that he was crying. You also noticed that his parent was very angry. (S)he handed you a manila envelope and said, "These are just the beginning of the bills you're going to have to pay for your dog biting my son!" (S)he told you that Benji had stuck his head through the fence and bitten Mark. The hospital bills were $3,500, and your neighbor said that Mark would need plastic surgery as well. (S)he stuck the envelope in your hand and stomped off with no other comment.

You feel sorry for Mark, but you don't believe the story. For one thing, Benji could not stick his head through the fence to bite someone. There has to be some other explanation. You suspect that Mark entered your yard, or perhaps stuck his arm through the fence, maybe to pet Benji.

The next morning, you received a visit from Animal Control. They impounded Benji to be observed for rabies. (Benji has since been returned in good health.) Right after this incident, you called your insurance agent, and he strongly advised mediation.

Role Two:

Please do not read the other player's role.

You live in a nice area in the North Valley with your spouse and your son Mark, who is 12 years old. You like this neighborhood very much and get along well with your neighbors. Your yard is separated from the neighbors to the south by a fence, which is about 5 feet tall. The fence is constructed of large-square wire mesh attached to wooden posts. It was constructed by your neighbor, but you have enjoyed the fence, which supports ivy and other climbing floral plants.

You do not know these neighbors very well, but Mark has often played with their son Tim, who is also 12. One Saturday a couple of weeks ago, Mark came screaming into the house. His arm was a bloody mess, with a seven-inch laceration running from the wrist up his forearm. You quickly wrapped the arm in a towel and jumped into the car to rush to the emergency room. Through his tears, Mark choked out that Benji, the neighbor's beagle, had stuck his head through the fence and grabbed Mark's arm. You were furious.

At the emergency room, the doctor cleaned and stitched the wound (32 stitches in all) and gave Mark a tetanus shot. The doctor also told you that there might be a scar after the arm heals, but unwanted scars can usually be removed by plastic surgery. When you left the emergency room, you were shocked to see that the bill was $3,500! You calmed down a little when you realized that insurance would cover most of this.

On the way home, Mark told you more about what happened. He was playing along the fence with some toy cars, and Benji just stuck his head right through and bit him. "He is such a mean dog," Mark told you. You were very upset and angry that a neighbor could harbor such a vicious animal. You felt you needed to make a strong statement to them and decided to do two things. First, you would report them to the police, and second, you would make them pay the medical bills!

You did call the police, but they referred you to Animal Control. To your satisfaction, Animal Control came right out the next day and took the dog away from them. (You were disappointed, however, that they ended up returning the dog a few days later.)

As for the bills, you and Mark marched right over there when you got back from the hospital and presented them with the bills. Even though you have insurance, you know that this family is rich and can afford it. Besides, the principle of the matter is important to you, and they should have to pay. Just to make the point even stronger, you let them know clearly that there may be more bills in the future, even the possibility of plastic surgery.

To your surprise, you have received a call from your neighbor suggesting mediation about this matter. You are not sure what mediation involves, but you want them to know the harm they have done to your son, so you agree to go.

The Termination Case

Role One:

Please do not read the other player's role.

You are Director of Plant Operations for Melville Community College. The college has grown rapidly over the past few years and several new buildings have been constructed. The workload for your department has increased substantially, and you feel that the budget has not kept pace with the increased workload. The custodial department has been especially hard hit, with the seven janitors having to take on additional buildings in their cleaning schedules. This has been painful for you because you came up through custodial services and were supervisor there prior to your promotion to director three years ago.

The custodial department has had other problems too. After your promotion, you hired a new supervisor, Jerry Padilla. He came highly recommended, and you were very pleased with his record. You wanted someone to take control of custodial services, and you have not been disappointed. He has been highly conscientious and loyal. You have gained a lot of confidence in his ability to supervise.

Almost from the beginning of his employment, though, Mr. Padilla has complained to you that several janitors are not doing as good a job as he thinks they should. He said that he often needs to ask them to correct their work. You have noticed that the annual performance reviews have been quite a bit lower than the ones you wrote when you were supervisor. You have not let this bother you, however, because you see it as a sign that Mr. Padilla has high standards, which is good.

Mr. Padilla identified one custodian as a particular problem. He said that this janitor was too slow and missed a lot of detail in the work. He said that he had spoken on several occasions to this custodian, but that the quality of the work had not improved. About four months ago, Mr. Padilla approached you about terminating this employee. You were especially troubled by this because the employee in question was one of your former workmates, and you liked him (her). His work was never outstanding, but (s)he did an adequate, if slow, job. You had even developed something of a friendship and frequently took breaks together. You have seen very little of him (her) since your promotion.

You did not want to undercut the confidence you have shown in the new supervisor and felt that you were hardly in a position to override his decision. You told him that he had the authority to fire the employee, but you cautioned him to be careful and make sure that the work performance was well documented. Padilla went ahead with the termination, and the employee almost immediately filed an EEOC complaint on the basis of age and disability.

You had been aware that the employee was "older," but you had not been aware of any disability. You felt that the age would not be a problem because the poor quality of work had been documented, and the employee was eligible to retire if (s)he chose. The disability is another matter, and you wish you had known about this before the termination. You asked Mr. Padilla about the disability, and he said that he was not aware of any disability.

The Human Resources Department has designated you to represent the college as responding party in this case. To your surprise, the local EEOC office has contacted you saying that the former employee is willing to enter mediation on the case and is inquiring as to whether the college would be willing to do likewise. After conferring with Human Resources, you decide to go forth with the mediation, and the college has given you full authority to negotiate a settlement in the case.

Role Two:

Please do not read the other player's role.

You have filed an EEOC complaint against your former employer Melville Community College for discrimination based on age and disability. You were let go after 16 years of service as a custodian for "failure to perform duties in a satisfactory manner." You are 57 years old and out of work. After your departure, you were replaced by a 34-year-old. You have applied for several custodial positions but haven't received any job offers, and you suspect that you are getting bad references from your former employer.

Up until about 3 years ago, you had gotten along well at work. You had become friends with your supervisor and often took breaks together. But things changed when your supervisor got promoted to Director of Plant Operations, and the college hired a new custodial supervisor, Jerry Padilla. Since then you have not seen much of your old supervisor, the new director.

From the beginning, Jerry seemed very critical of your work. He frequently pointed out little jobs he wanted to you to do over again. These almost always seemed petty and unreasonable, but you did not want to make waves, so you just did what he said. Until the new supervisor arrived, your annual performance reviews were "satisfactory-to-good," but the two annual reviews conducted by your new supervisor were more in the "fair-to-satisfactory" category. You have been upset about this, but you didn't know what you could do about it and certainly never expected to be fired.

To make matters worse, about three months before you were fired, your supervisor added a new building to your work schedule. You were already responsible for three buildings, and this made a fourth. He said that the budget was not sufficient to keep custodial services in line with new building construction and that workloads would need to be increased. The new building is some distance away and up a steep hill from the other buildings on your schedule. You now suspect that your supervisor increased your workload to force you to quit.

The added workload is especially difficult for you because you have an arthritic ankle, which has been getting increasingly painful. Your janitorial work is not as easy as it used to be, and you find walking and carrying difficult. You have been a janitor all of your life, and this recent flare-up of arthritis is disconcerting to you. You really want to keep working, but you worry that the disability will someday make it impossible to keep doing this kind of work. However, you feel that you can still do the work, and the firing implied that you are no longer able to perform up to standards. You have many years of experience, know how to do the work very well, and care about doing the job right. You have noticed that many of the younger janitors are sloppy and careless, and they don't seem to care about the quality of the work as you do.

You do qualify for retirement, but at age 57 with only 16 years of service, your pension would be small, and you are not ready to retire. You are comfortable at Melville College and would like to return to work there, although you would hate to be assigned to the same supervisor. You realize you are not as fast as you used to be and would like an accommodation for your disability. You were pleased to learn that you could go to mediation over your case and have agreed to do so because you feel certain that the college will reinstate you if they hear your side of the story. You are also pleased to learn that your old supervisor, the director of plant operations, will be representing the college in your mediation.

Guidelines for Mediation Coaching

1. Begin with the positive. Look for the things the trainee did well and acknowledge this.
   Helen, your introduction was superb! All of the elements were present, and I really liked the conversational and informal tone.
2. State criticism constructively. Rather than identifying what the trainee did poorly, suggest changes or improvements that he or she might consider in the future.
   Taylor, I noticed that you gave each disputant a full opportunity to tell his or her story without interrupting. I liked that, but I wonder if next time you might consider giving a couple of little summaries during this process.
3. Be specific.
   Morgan, you handled the brainstorming really well. I especially liked the way in which you kept the ideas flowing and noticed that when you did this the disputants forgot about their animosities.
4. Find the seeds for improvement in what the trainee did. Start with what was done and show how this is a step in the right direction; then explain how the action could be improved.
   Molly, I liked it when you acknowledged Bill's desire to get custody of the dog. That shows good listening and can help him feel understood. Now just take it one step further and try to include a reflection of Bill's feeling as well as the content of his message. I think he was feeling very sad about losing his pet.
5. Admit your own perspective and acknowledge that different mediators and coaches might see things differently.
   In my practice, I am more comfortable minimizing the introduction because I don't like to structure the process too much at the beginning, but other mediators prefer a fuller introduction. Try it both ways and decide for yourself.
6. Provide explanations. Reveal your reasoning and rationale.
   I liked your problem-solving work, and this will serve you well in many mediations. For myself, though, I don't like to begin problem solving quite so quickly because I think it is important to take time to see where the disputants' relationship is going and the kind of work they seem to want to do.

7. Check trainee perceptions. Ask them how they felt about the process and provide time for them to explore their perceptions.
   Ralph, I was wondering about that suggestion you made regarding keeping the doors locked. For me, that seemed to be leading, but I wonder what you were trying to do there.
8. Allow opportunity to pursue trainee concerns.
   Before we get started, did you have any questions or concerns that you would like to talk about?

Co-Mediator Debriefing Form

(to use in discussing the session after completion)

1. How did we contribute to effective . . .
   Listening
   Acknowledgment
   Responding
   Commitment
2. When we did these things, how did they contribute to improving . . .
   Collaborative communication
   Power management
   Process management
   Face work
   Safe environment
3. When and how did we help the parties gain . . .
   Empowerment and recognition
   Community consciousness
   Commitment building
4. What might we have done differently to help the parties listen, acknowledge, respond, and commit?
5. What might we have done differently to help the parties achieve the five characteristics of collaborative communication, power management, process management, face work, and safe environment?
6. What might we have done differently to help the parties achieve the three goals of empowerment and recognition, community consciousness, and commitment building?

Participant Survey

You recently participated in a mediation at the Community Mediation Center. We would appreciate your candid evaluation of this mediation session. Please answer each of the following questions by circling the appropriate response:

1. How effective were the mediators in helping the disputants work together to solve their problem?

Highly effective	Effective	No opinion	Ineffective	Very ineffective

2. To what extent were you given the opportunity to talk about what was important to you?

Much opportunity	Some opportunity	No opinion	Not much opportunity	None whatsoever

3. To what extent did the mediators give you an opportunity to help determine the process that was used in the mediation?

A great deal	Some	No opinion	Very little	None

4. How well did the mediators work to build respect within the mediation?

They worked very hard at this	They tried somewhat	No opinion	They did very little	There was no effort at all

5. To what extent did the mediators help build a safe environment in this session?

They did a lot	They worked somewhat	No opinion	They did very little	There was no effort at all

6. What is your general evaluation of this mediation?

Excellent	Adequate	No opinion	Inadequate	Poor

Please write any comments you might have about this mediation:

Mediation Observation Form

This form (on the following page) is designed to assist you in observing mediations. It can be used in role plays or actual mediation situations. The form has the advantage of focusing on mediation goals and conflict management characteristics, which provide thematic continuity to your observation. In other words, instead of observing isolated behavior, you will be looking at how behaviors connect to one another and what is being "made" or "constructed" in the process.

As you observe, note the specific mediator behaviors you see. Check these off in the column on the left. Do not worry about finding everything in the checklist because mediators do not always use every technique. If you see techniques not listed, write them in the blank spaces at the bottom. More than noting the behavior, however, see how it relates to the goals and characteristics. To prepare for the observation, you may wish to review the goals in chapter 5 and the characteristics in chapter 3.

You will probably not be able to fit all your insights on this form, so you may wish to use notebook paper for more complete notes. We encourage you to make a photocopied enlargement of the page on 11"× 17" paper so that you have a large "chart" with which to work.

Mediation Observation Form

Mediator Behaviors

- ☐ Acknowledging
- ☐ Active listening
- ☐ Agenda setting
- ☐ Agreement writing
- ☐ Caucusing
- ☐ Clarifying
- ☐ Closing the session
- ☐ Defining the problem
- ☐ Encouraging
- ☐ Establishing criteria
- ☐ Establishing guidelines
- ☐ Explaining the process
- ☐ Identifying interests
- ☐ Introducing mediation
- ☐ Inviting options
- ☐ Issue identification
- ☐ Questioning
- ☐ Reality testing
- ☐ Reflecting
- ☐ Reframing
- ☐ Remaining neutral
- ☐ Restating
- ☐ Summarizing
- ☐
- ☐
- ☐

Mediation Goals	How did the mediator(s) help achieve this goal?	How did the mediator(s) detract from achieving this goal?
Empowerment and Recognition Community Consciousness Commitment Building		

Conflict Management Characteristics	How did the mediator(s) help create this characteristic?	How did the mediator(s) detract from this characteristic?
Collaborative Communication Power Management Process Management Facework Safe Environment		

References

Barry, A. M. (2009). Mirror neurons: How we become what we see. *Visual Communication Quarterly, 16*(2), 79–89.

Bohannan, P. (1992). *We, the alien: An introduction to cultural anthropology.* Long Grove, IL: Waveland Press.

Booth, D., & Hachiya, M. (Eds.). (2004). *The arts go to school: Classroom-based activities that focus on music, painting, drama, movement, media, and more*. Pembroke Publishers Limited.

Bush, R. A. B., & Folger, J. P. (1994). *The promise of mediation: Responding to conflict through empowerment and recognition.* San Francisco: Jossey-Bass.

Carter, J. (1993). *Talking peace: A vision for the next generation.* New York: Penguin.

Crum, T. F. (1987). *The magic of conflict.* New York: Simon & Schuster.

Donohue, W. A., & Kolt, R. (1992). *Managing interpersonal conflict.* Newbury Park: Sage.

Fagre, L. (1995). Recognizing disputant's face-needs in community mediation. Paper presented at Western States Communication Association Conference.

Fisher, R., & Ury, W. (1991). *Getting to yes: Negotiating agreement without giving in* (2nd ed.). New York: Penguin.

Grant, J. Mediator, University of New Mexico Mediation Clinic, Albuquerque, NM.

Gray, B. (2004). Strong opposition: frame-based resistance to collaboration. *Journal of Community & Applied Social Psychology, 14*(3), 166–176.

Hocker, J., & Wilmot, W. (2001). *Interpersonal conflict* (6th ed.). Dubuque, IA: W. C. Brown.

Hughes, S. (1998, Winter). A closer look: The case for a mediation confidentiality privilege still has not been made. *Dispute Resolution Magazine, 5*, 14–16.

Katsh, E. (2007). Online dispute resolution: Some implications for the emergence of law in cyberspace. *International Review of Law Computers & Technology, 21*(2), 97–107.

Kaufman, G., & Raphael, L. (1983). *The dynamics of power: Building a competent self.* Rochester, VT: Schenkman Books.

Kolb, D. M., & Associates. (1994). *When talk works: Profiles of mediators.* San Francisco: Jossey-Bass.

Kritek, P. B. (1994). *Negotiating at an uneven table: Developing moral courage in resolving our conflicts.* San Francisco: Jossey-Bass.

Lakoff, G., & Johnson, M. (1980). *Metaphors we live by.* Chicago: University of Chicago Press.

Lilley, R. C. (2006). *Dealing with difficult people* (Vol. 8). Kogan Page Publishers.

Littlejohn, S. W., & Domenici, K. (2007). *Communication, conflict, and the management of difference.* Long Grove, IL: Waveland Press.

Littlejohn, S. W., Shailor, J., & Pearce, W. B. (1994). The deep structure of reality in mediation. In J. P. Folger & T. S. Jones (Eds.), *New directions in mediation* (pp. 67–83). Thousand Oaks, CA: Sage.

Lulofs, R. S. (1994). *Conflict: From theory to action.* Scottsdale, AZ: Gorsuch Scarisbrick.

Mehrabian, A. (2017). *Nonverbal communication.* New York: Routledge.

Moore, C. (1986). *The mediation process: Practical strategies for resolving conflict.* San Francisco: Jossey-Bass. See also 2nd ed., 1996.

Moore, C. W. (2014). *The mediation process: Practical strategies for resolving conflict.* John Wiley & Sons.

Moreno, J. L., & Moreno, Z. T. (1946). *Psychodrama.* New York: Beacon House.

Olson, C. (1994). *Basic meeting facilitation skills training.* Albuquerque: Cynthia Olson & Associates.

Pearce, W. B. (1994). *Interpersonal communication: Making social worlds.* New York: HarperCollins.

Pearce, W. B., & Pearce, K. A. (1999). Combining passions and abilities: Toward dialogic virtuosity. *Southern Communication Journal, 65*, 161–175.

Srivastva, S., & Cooperrider, D. L. (1999). *Appreciative management and leadership.* Euclid, OH: Williams Custom Publishing.

Sunoo, J. J. (1990, October). Some rules of thumb for intercultural mediators. *Negotiation Journal, 6*, 388–390.

Thomas, A. (1991). *Making the tough calls: Ethical exercises for neutral dispute resolvers*. Eagle, NE: Association for Conflict Resolution.

Ury, W. (2000). *The third side: Why we fight and how we can stop*. New York: Penguin.

Verderber, R. F., & Verderber, K. S. (1992). *Inter-act: Using interpersonal communication skills*. Belmont, CA: Wadswsorth. See also 9th ed., 2001.

Wilmot, W., Hocker, J., Arthur, J., Petty, J. W., Martocchio, J. J., Cheeseman, H. R., . . . & Rosania, R. J. (2007). *Interpersonal conflict*, 9th ed. New York: McGraw-Hill.

Wilson, S. R., & Putnam, L. L. (1990). Interaction goals in negotiation. In James A. Anderson (Ed.), *Communication yearbook 13* (pp. 374–406). Newbury Park, CA: Sage.

Wolvin, A., & Coakley, C. G. (1992). *Listening*. Dubuque, IA: W. C. Brown. See also 5th ed., 1996, McGraw-Hill.

Suggested Reading

Abel, R. L. (1982). *The politics of informal justice*. New York: Academic Press.

Alger, C., & Stohl, M. (Eds.). (1988). *A just peace through transformation: Cultural, economic, and political foundations for change*. Boulder, CO: Westview Press.

Allen, M., Donohue, W., & Stewart, B. (1990). Comparing hardline and softline bargaining strategies in zero-sum situations using meta-analysis. In M. A. Rahim (Ed.), *Theory and research in conflict management* (pp. 86–103). New York: Praeger.

Allison, G. T., Carnesale, A., & Nye, J. S., Jr. (Eds.) (1985). *Hawks, doves and owls: An agenda for avoiding nuclear war*. New York: W. W. Norton.

Allison, G. T., Ury, W. L., & Allyn, B. J. (1989). *Windows of opportunity: From cold war to peaceful competition in U.S.–Soviet relations*. Cambridge, MA: Ballinger.

Antilla, S. (1995, February 5). The next magic bullet? Mediation. *The New York Times*, section 3, p. 13.

Assefa, H. (1987). *Mediation of civil wars: Approaches and strategies—The Sudan conflict*. Boulder, CO: Westview Press.

Auerbach, J. (1983). *Justice without law?* New York: Oxford University Press.

Axelrod, R. (1984). *The evolution of cooperation.* New York: Basic Books.
Bacharach, S. B. (1983). Bargaining within organizations. In M. H. Bazerman & R. J. Lewicki (Eds.), *Negotiating in organizations* (pp. 360–376). Beverly Hills: Sage.
Bacharach, S. B., & Lawler, E. J. (1980). Power and politics in organizations. In *The social psychology of conflict, coalitions, and bargaining.* San Francisco: Jossey-Bass.
Bacharach, S. B., & Lawler, E. J. (1981). *Bargaining: Power, tactics and outcomes.* San Francisco: Jossey-Bass.
Bacharach, S. B., & Lawler, E. J. (1986). Power dependence and power paradoxes in bargaining. *Negotiation Journal, 2,* 167–174.
Bacow, L. S., & Wheeler, M. (1984). *Environmental dispute resolution.* New York: Plenum Press.
Bart, J., Beisecker, T., & Walker, G. (1989). Knowledge versus ignorance as bargaining strategies: The impact of knowledge about other's information level. *The Social Science Journal, 26*(2), 161–172.
Bartos, O. J. (1974). *Process and outcome of negotiations.* New York: Columbia University Press.
Bazerman, M. H., & Carroll, J. S. (1987). Negotiator cognition. In L. L. Cummings & B. M. Staw (Eds.), *Research in organizational behavior, 9* (pp. 247–288). Greenwich, CT: JAI Press.
Bercovitch, J. (1992, April). Mediators and mediation strategies in international relations. *Negotiation Journal, 8,* 99–112.
Bernard, S. E., Folger, J. P., Weingarten, H. R., & Zumeta, Z. R. (1984). The neutral mediator: Value dilemmas in divorce mediation. *Mediation Quarterly, 4,* 49–60.
Bies, R. J., Shapiro, D. L., & Cummings, L. L. (1988). Causal accounts and managing organizational conflict. *Communication Research Special Issue: Communication, Conflict and Dispute Resolution, 15,* 381–399.
Bigoness, W. J., & Kesner, I. F. (1986). Mediation effectiveness: What can we learn from leadership research. In R. J. Lewicki, B. H. Sheppard, & M. H. Bazerman (Eds.), *Research on negotiation in organizations, Vol. 1* (pp. 229–249). Greenwich, CT: JAI Press.
Blake, R., & Mouton, J. S. (1984). *Solving costly organizational conflicts.* San Francisco: Jossey-Bass.
Blalock, H. M., Jr. (1989). *Power and conflict: Toward a general theory.* Newbury Park, CA: Sage.
Boehringer, G. H., Zeruolis, V., Bayley, J., & Boehringer, K. (1974). Stirling: The destructive application of group techniques to a conflict. *Journal of Conflict Resolution, 18,* 257–275.

Bowser, B. P., Auletta, G. S., & Jones, T. (1993). *Confronting diversity issues on campus*. Newbury Park, CA: Sage.

Braiker, H. B., & Kelley, H. H. (1979). Conflict in the development of close relationships. In R. L. Burgess & T. L. Huston (Eds.), *Social exchange in developing relationships* (pp. 135–168). New York: Academic Press.

Brett, M., Drieghe, R., & Shapiro, D. L. (1986). Mediator style and mediation effectiveness. *Negotiation Journal, 2,* 277–286.

Brookmire, D. A., & Sistruck, F. (1980). The effects of perceived ability and impartiality of mediators and time pressure on negotiations. *Journal of Conflict Resolution, 24,* 311–327.

Brown, L. D. (1992). Normative conflict management theories: Past, present, and future. *Journal of Organizational Behavior, 13,* 303–309.

Burrell, N. A., Donohue, W. A., & Allen, M. (1988). Gender-based perceptual bias in mediation. *Communication Research Special Issue: Communication, Conflict and Dispute Resolution, 15,* 447–469.

Burrell, N. A., Donohue, W. A., & Allen, M. (1990). The impact of disputants' expectations on mediation: Testing an interventionist model. *Human Communication Research, 17,* 104–139.

Bush, R. A., & Folger, J. P. (1994). *The promise of mediation: Responding to conflict through empowerment and recognition.* San Francisco: Jossey-Bass.

Cahn, D. D. (1990). Intimates in conflict: A research review. In D. Cahn (Ed.), *Intimates in conflict: A communication perspective* (pp. 1–24). Hillsdale, NJ: Lawrence Erlbaum.

Carnevale, P. J. D. (1986). Mediating disputes and decisions in organizations. In R. J. Lewicki, B. H. Sheppard, & M. H. Bazerman (Eds.), *Research on negotiation in organizations, Vol. 1* (pp. 251–269). Greenwich, CT: JAI Press.

Carnevale, P. J. D. (1986). Strategic choice in mediation. *Negotiation Journal, 2,* 41–56.

Carnevale, P., & Pegnetter, R. (1985). The selection of mediation tactics in public sector disputes: A contingency analysis. *Journal of Social Issues, 41,* 65–81.

Cobb, S. (1994). A narrative perspective on mediation: Toward the materialization of the "storytelling" metaphor, orientations to conflict, and mediation discourse. In J. P. Folger & T. S. Jones (Eds.), *New directions in mediation* (pp. 48–63). Thousand Oaks, CA: Sage.

Cohen, H. (1980). *You can negotiate anything*. Secaucus, NJ: Lyle Stuart.

Comstock, J., & Buller, D. B. (1991). Conflict strategies adolescents use with their parents: Testing the cognitive communicator characteristics model. *Journal of Language and Social Psychology, 10,* 47–60.

Corcoran, K. O., & Melamed, J. C. (1989). From coercion to empowerment: Spousal abuse and mediation. *Mediation Quarterly, 7,* 303–316.

Courtright, J. A., Millar, F. E., Rogers, L. E., & Bagarozzi, D. (1990). Interaction dynamics of relational negotiation: Reconciliation versus termination of distressed relationships. *Western Journal of Speech Communication, 154,* 429–453.

Cushman, D. P., & King, S. S. (1985). National and organizational cultures in conflict resolution: Japan, the United States, and Yugoslavia. In W. B. Gudykunst, L. P. Stewart, & S. Ting-Toomey (Eds.), *Communication, culture, and organizational processes* (pp. 114–133). Beverly Hills: Sage.

Davidow, J. (1979). *A peace in southern Africa: The Lancaster house, conference on Rhodesia.* Boulder, CO: Westview Press.

Davis, A. M., & Salem, R. A. (1984). Dealing with power imbalances in the mediation of interpersonal disputes. *Mediation Quarterly, 6,* 17–26.

De Waal, F. (1994). Conflict resolution. In J. J. Bonsignore, E. Katsh, P. d'Errico, R. M. Pipkin, S. Arons, & J. Rifkin (Eds.), *Before the law: An introduction to the legal process* (5th ed., pp. 485–486). Palo Alto, CA: Houghton Mifflin.

Deetz, S. (1990). Reclaiming the subject matter as a guide to mutual understanding: Effectiveness and ethics in interpersonal interaction. *Communication Quarterly, 38,* 226–243.

DeStephen, D. (1987, November). Mediating power imbalances: The mediator's responsibility to protect disputants from unfair solutions. Paper presented at the annual convention of the Speech Communication Association, Boston, MA.

Deutsch, M. (1973). *The resolution of conflict: Constructive and destructive processes.* New Haven, CT: Yale University Press.

Diez, M. E. (1986). Negotiation competence: A conceptualization of the rules of negotiation interaction. In D. G. Ellis & W. A. Donohue (Eds.), *Contemporary issues in language and discourse processes* (pp. 223–238). Hillsdale, NJ: Lawrence Erlbaum.

Donohue, W. A. (1981). Analyzing negotiation tactics: Development of a negotiation interact system. *Human Communication Research, 7,* 273–287.

Donohue, W. A. (1989). Communication competence in mediators. In K. Kressel & D. G. Pruitt (Eds.), *Mediation research: The process and effectiveness of third-party intervention* (pp. 322–342). San Francisco: Jossey-Bass.

Donohue, W. A. (1991). *Communication, marital dispute and divorce mediation.* Hillsdale, NJ: Lawrence Erlbaum.

Donohue, W. A., Allen, M., & Burrell, N. (1988). Mediator communicative competence. *Communication Monographs, 55,* 104–119.

Donohue, W. A., & Bresnahan, M. L (1994). Communication issues in mediating cultural conflict. In J. P. Folger & T. S. Jones (Eds.), *New directions in mediation* (pp. 135–158). Thousand Oaks, CA: Sage.

Donohue, W. A., Diez, M. E., & Hamilton, M. (1984). Coding naturalistic negotiation interaction. *Human Communication Research, 10,* 403–425.

Donohue, W., & Kolt, R. (1994). *Managing interpersonal conflict.* Newbury Park, CA: Sage.

Donohue, W. A., Ramesh, C., Kaufman, G., & Smith, R. (1991). Crisis bargaining in intense conflict situations. *International Journal of Group Tendencies, 21,* 133–145.

Donohue, W. A., & Roberto, A. (1993). Relational developments as negotiated order in hostage negotiation. *Human Communication Research, 20*(2), 175–198.

Druckman, D., Broome, B. J., & Korper, S. H. (1988). Value differences and conflict resolution: Facilitation or delinking? *Journal of Conflict Resolution, 32*(3), 489–510.

Elkouri, F., & Elkouri, E. A. (1985). *How arbitration works* (4th ed.). Washington, DC: Bureau of National Affairs.

Ellis, D. G., & Fisher, B. A. (1975). Phases of conflict in small group development: A Markov analysis. *Human Communication Research, 1,* 195 212.

Emond, P. (Ed.). (1989). *Commercial dispute resolution: Alternatives to litigation.* Aurora, Ontario, Canada: Law Books.

Feuille, P. (1992). Why does grievance mediation resolve grievances? *Negotiation Journal, 8*(2), 131–145.

Feuille, P., & Kolb, D. (1994). Waiting in the wings: Mediation's role in grievance resolution. *Negotiation Journal, 10*(3), 249–264.

Fisher, G. (1980). *International negotiation: A cross-cultural perspective.* Chicago: Intercultural Press.

Fisher, R. J. (1969). *International conflict for beginners.* New York: Harper and Row.

Fisher, R. J. (1972). *Dear Israelis, dear Arabs: A working approach to peace.* New York: Harper and Row.

Fisher, R. J. (1978). *International mediation: A workshop guide.* New York: International Peace Academy.

Fisher, R. J. (1983). Third party consultation as a method of intergroup conflict resolution. *Journal of Conflict Resolution, 27*(2), 301–334.

Fisher, R. J. (1985). Beyond yes. *Negotiation Journal, 2,* 67–70.

Fisher, R. J. (1994). *Beyond Machiavelli: Tools for coping with conflict.* Cambridge, MA: Harvard University Press.

Fisher, R., & Ury, W. (1991). *Getting to yes: Negotiation agreement without giving in* (2nd ed.). New York: Penguin Books.

Folberg, J. P., & Taylor, A. (1993). *Mediation: A comprehensive guide to resolving conflicts without litigation.* San Francisco: Jossey-Bass.

Folger, J. P., & Bush, R. A. B. (1994). Ideology, orientations to conflict, and mediation discourse. In J. P. Folger & T. S. Jones (Eds.), *New directions in mediation* (pp. 3–25). Thousand Oaks, CA: Sage.

Folger, J. P., & Jones, T. S. (Eds.). (1994). *New directions in mediation.* Thousand Oaks, CA: Sage.

Folger, J. P., & Poole, M. S. (2001). *Working through conflict: A communication perspective* (4th ed.). New York: Longman.

Folger, R. (1986). Mediation, arbitration, and the psychology of procedural justice. In R. J. Lewicki, B. H. Sheppard, & M. H. Bazerman (Eds.), *Research on negotiation in organizations, Vol. 1* (pp. 57–59). Greenwich, CT: JAI Press.

Foss, S. K., & Foss, K. A. (2019). *Inviting transformation: Presentational speaking for a changing world* (4th ed.). Long Grove, IL: Waveland Press.

Freeman, S. A., Littlejohn, S. W., & Pearce, W. B. (1992). Communication and moral conflict. *Western Journal of Communication, 56*(4), 311–329.

Fuller, A. A. (1994). Conflict resolution: Bane or boost to peace and justice? In J. J. Bonsignore, E. Katsh, P. d'Errico, R. M. Pipkin, S. Arons, & J. Rifkin (Eds.), *Before the law: An introduction to the legal process* (5th ed., pp. 512–514). Palo Alto, CA: Houghton Mifflin.

Gadlin, H. (1991). Careful maneuvers: Mediating sexual harassment. *Negotiation Journal, 7*(2), 139–153.

Gilligan, C. (1982). *In a different voice: Psychological theory and women's development.* Cambridge, MA: Harvard University Press.

Goffman, E. (1959). *The presentation of self in everyday life.* Garden City, NY: Doubleday.

Gold, L. (1985). Reflections on the transition from therapist to mediator. *Mediation Quarterly, 9,* 15–26.

Goldberg, S. B. (1989). Grievance mediation: A successful alternative to labor arbitration. *Negotiation Journal, 5*(1), 9–15.

Goldberg, S. B., Green, E., & Sander, F. (1995). *Dispute resolution.* Boston, MA: Little, Brown.

Hale, C. L., Bast, C., & Gordon, B. (1991, April). Communication within a dispute mediation: Interactants' perceptions of the process. *The International Journal of Conflict Management, 2*(2), 139–158.

Hall, E. T. (1983). *Dance of life.* New York: Anchor Books. Helm, B. (1989). Mediators' duties, informed consent and the

Helm, B. (1988). Mediators' duties, informed consent and the Hatfields versus the McCoys. *Mediation Quarterly, 21,* 65–75.

Helm, B., & Scott, S. (1986). Advocacy in mediation. *Mediation Quarterly, 13,* 69–76.

Hiltrop, J. M. (1989). Factors associated with successful labor mediation. In K. Kressel & D. Pruitt (Eds.), *Mediation research: The process and effectiveness of third-party intervention* (pp. 241–262). San Francisco: Jossey-Bass.

Himes, J. S. (1980). *Conflict and conflict management.* Athens: University of Georgia Press.

Ippolito, C. A., & Pruitt, D. G. (1990). Power balancing in mediation: Outcomes and implications of mediator intervention. *The International Journal of Conflict Management, 1,* 341–356.

Jones, T. S. (1988). Phase structures in agreement and no-agreement mediation. *Communication Research Special Issue: Communication, Conflict and Dispute Resolution, 15,* 470–495.

Jones, T. S., & Brinkman, H. (1994). Teach your children well: Recommendations for peer mediation programs. In J. P. Folger & T. S. Jones (Eds.), *New directions in mediation* (pp. 159–174). Thousand Oaks, CA: Sage.

Kanitz, M. A. (1987). *Getting apart together: The couple's guide to a fair divorce or separation.* San Luis Obispo, CA: Impact.

Karambayya, R., & Brett, J. M. (1994). Managerial third parties: Intervention strategies, process, and consequences. In J. P. Folger & T. S. Jones (Eds.), *New directions in mediation* (pp. 175–192). Thousand Oaks, CA: Sage.

Kelly, C., & Troester, R. (1991). *Peacemaking through communication.* Annandale, VA: Speech Communication Association.

Kelman, H. C. (1994). Interactive problem-solving: A social-psychological approach to conflict resolution. In J. J. Bon-signore, E. Katsh, P. d'Errico, R. M. Pipkin, S. Arons, & J. Rifkin (Eds.), *Before the law: An introduction to the legal process* (5th ed., pp. 507–510). Palo Alto, CA: Houghton Mifflin.

Keltner, J. W. (1994). *The management of struggle: Elements of dispute resolution through negotiation, mediation and arbitration.* Cresskill, NJ: Hampton Press.

King, W. C., Jr., & Miles, E. W. (1990). What we know—and don't know—about measuring conflict: An examination of the ROCI-11 and the OCCI conflict instruments. *Management Communication Quarterly, 4,* 222–243.

Klingel, S., & Martin, A. (Eds.). (1988). *A fighting chance: New strategies to save jobs and reduce costs.* Ithaca, NY: ILR Press.

Knapp, M. L., Putnam, L. L., & Davis, L. J. (1988). Measuring interpersonal conflict in organizations: Where do we go from here. *Management Communication Quarterly, 1,* 414–429.

Knebel, F., & Clay, G. S. (1987). *Before you sue: How to get justice without going to court.* New York: Morrow.

Kolb, D. M. (1983). *The mediators.* Cambridge, MA: MIT Press.

Kolb, D. M. (1983). Strategy and the tactics of mediation. *Human Relations, 36,* 247–268.

Kolb, D. M. (1985). To be a mediator: Expressive tactics in mediation. *Journal of Social Issues, 41,* 11–26.

Kolb, D. M. (1989). Labor mediators, managers, and ombudsmen: Roles mediators play in different contexts. In K. Kressel & D. G. Pruitt (Eds.), *Mediation research: The process and effectiveness of third-party intervention* (pp. 91–114). San Francisco: Jossey-Bass.

Kolb, D. M. & Associates. (1994). *When talk works: Profiles of mediators.* San Francisco: Jossey-Bass.

Kolb, D. M., & Glidden, P. A. (1986). Getting to know your conflict options. *Personnel Administrator, 31,* 77–89.

Kolb, D. M., & Putnam, L. L. (1992). The multiple faces of conflict in organizations. In R. J. Lewicki, B. H. Sheppard, & M. H. Bazerman (Eds.), *Research on negotiation in organizations, Vol. 1* (pp. 57–59). Greenwich, CT: JAI Press.

Kolb, D. M., & Silbey, S. S. (1990). Enhancing the capacity of organizations to deal with disputes. *Negotiation Journal, 6,* 297–304.

Kramer, V. (1992). Mediation: Perils, pitfalls and benefits. *Mothering, 65,* 100–106.

Kressel, K. (1972). *Labor mediation: An exploratory survey.* Albany, NY: Association of Labor Mediation Agencies.

Kressel, K. (1985). *The process of divorce: How professionals and couples negotiate settlements.* New York: Basic Books.

Kressel, K., & Pruitt, D. (1989). *Mediation research: The process and effectiveness of third-party intervention.* San Francisco: Jossey-Bass.

Kritek, P. B. (1994). *Negotiating at an uneven table: Developing moral courage in resolving our conflicts.* San Francisco: Jossey-Bass.

Lannamann, J. W. (1991). Interpersonal communication research as ideological practice. *Communication Theory, 1,* 179–203.

Lax, D. A., & Sebenius, J. K. (1985). The power of alternatives or the limits of negotiation. *Negotiation Journal, 1,* 163–180.

Lax, D. A., & Sebenius, J. K. (1986). *The manager as negotiator: Bargaining for cooperation and competitive gain.* New York: The Free Press.

Leitch, M. L. (1987). The politics of compromise: A feminist perspective on mediation. *Mediation Quarterly, 15,* 163–176.

Levine, M. I. (1986). Power imbalances in dispute resolution. In E. Palenski & H. M. Launer (Eds.), *Mediation: Contexts and challenges* (pp. 63–76). Springfield, IL: Charles C. Thomas.

Lewicki, R. J., Weiss, S. E., & Lewin, D. (1992). Model of conflict, negotiation and third-party intervention: A review and synthesis. *Journal of Organizational Behavior, 13,* 209–252.

Littlejohn, S. W., & Domenici, K. (2001). *Engaging communication in conflict: Systemic practice.* Thousand Oaks, CA: Sage Publications.

Littlejohn, S. W., Shailor, J., & Pearce, W. B. (1994). The deep structure of reality in mediation. In J. P. Folger & T. S. Jones (Eds.), *New directions in mediation* (pp. 67–83). Thousand Oaks, CA: Sage.

Lujan, D. (1994). The quality of justice. In J. J. Bonsignore, E. Katsh, P. d'Errico, R. M. Pipkin, S. Arons, & J. Rifkin (Eds.), *Before the law: An introduction to the legal process* (5th ed., pp. 514–515). Palo Alto, CA: Houghton Mifflin.

Lulofs, R. S. (1994). *Conflict: From theory to action.* Scottsdale, AZ: Gorsuch Scarisbrick.

Mayer, B. (1987). The dynamics of power in mediation and negotiation. *Mediation Quarterly, 16,* 75–86.

McEwen, C. A., & Maiman, R. J. (1989). Mediation in small claims court: Consensual processes and outcomes. In K. Kressel & D. G. Pruitt (Eds.), *Mediation research: The process and effectiveness of third-party intervention* (pp. 53–67). San Francisco: Jossey-Bass.

Merry, S. E. (1989). Mediation in nonindustrial societies. In K. Kressel & D. G. Pruitt (Eds.), *Mediation research: The process and effectiveness of third-party intervention* (pp. 53–67). San Francisco: Jossey-Bass.

Moore, C. W. (1994). Why do we mediate? In J. P. Folger & T. S. Jones (Eds.), *New directions in mediation* (pp. 195–203). Thousand Oaks, CA: Sage.

Moore, C. W. (1996). *The mediation process: Practical strategies for resolving conflict* (2nd ed.). San Francisco: Jossey-Bass.

Muldoon, B. (1993). *The heart of conflict.* New York: G. P. Putnam's Sons.

Nierenberg, G. I. (1968). *The art of negotiation.* New York: Cornerstone Library Publications.

Peachey, D. E. (1989). What people want from mediation. In K. Kressel & D. G. Pruitt (Eds.), *Mediation research: The process and effectiveness of third-party intervention* (pp. 300–321). San Francisco: Jossey-Bass.

Pearce, W. B., & Littlejohn, S. W. (1997). *Moral conflict: When social worlds collide.* Thousand Oaks: Sage Publications.

Pruitt, D. G., McGillicuddy, N. B., Welton, G. L., & Fry, W. R. (1989). Process of mediation in dispute settlement centers. In K. Kressel & D. G. Pruitt (Eds.), *Mediation research: The process and effectiveness of third-party intervention* (pp. 368–395). San Francisco: Jossey-Bass.

Putnam, L. L. (1988). Communication and interpersonal conflict in organizations. *Management Communication Quarterly, 1,* 293–301.

Putnam, L. L. (1989). Negotiation and organizing: Two levels within the Weickian model. *Communication Studies, 40,* 249–257.

Putnam, L. L. (1990). Reframing integrative and distributive bargaining: A process perspective. In B. H. Sheppard, M. H. Bazerman, & R. J. Lewicki (Eds.), *Research on negotiation in organizations, 2* (pp. 3–30). Greenwich, CT: JAI Press.

Putnam, L. L., & Folger, J. P. (1988). Communication, conflict, and dispute resolution: The study of interaction and the development of conflict theory. *Communication Research Special Issue: Communication, Conflict and Dispute Resolution, 15,* 349–360.

Rapoport, A., and Chammah, A. M. (1965). *Prisoner's dilemma.* Ann Arbor: University of Michigan Press.

Rifkin, J. (1994). Mediation from a feminist perspective: Promise and problems. In J. J. Bonsignore, E. Katsh, P. d'Errico, R. M. Pipkin, S. Arons, & J. Rifkin (Eds.), *Before the law: An introduction to the legal process* (5th ed., pp. 498–501). Palo Alto, CA: Houghton Mifflin.

Rifkin, J. (1994). The practitioner's dilemma. In J. P. Folger & T. S. Jones (Eds.), *New directions in mediation* (pp. 67–83). Thousand Oaks, CA: Sage.

Rifkin, J., & Katsh, E. (1994). Out of court. In J. J. Bonsignore, E. Katsh, P. d'Errico, R. M. Pipkin, S. Arons, & J. Rifkin (Eds.), *Before the law: An introduction to the legal process* (5th ed., pp. 495–498). Palo Alto, CA: Houghton Mifflin.

Rifkin, J., Millen, J., & Cobb, S. (1994). Toward a new discourse for mediation: A critique of neutrality. In J. J. Bon-signore, E. Katsh,

P. d'Errico, R. M. Pipkin, S. Arons, & J. Rifkin (Eds.), *Before the law: An introduction to the legal process* (5th ed., pp. 501–507). Palo Alto, CA: Houghton Mifflin.

Roehl, J., Royer, F., & Cook, R. (1989). Mediation in interpersonal disputes: Effectiveness and limitations. In K. Kressel & D. G. Pruitt (Eds.), *Mediation research: The process and effectiveness of third-party intervention* (pp. 44–68). San Francisco: Jossey-Bass.

Rogers, N., & McEwen, C. (1989). *Mediation: Law, policy, practice.* New York: The Lawyers Cooperative.

Rogers, N., & Salem, R. (1987). *A student's guide to mediation and the law.* New York: Matthew Bender.

Rothman, J. (1989). Supplementing tradition: A theoretical and practical typology for international conflict management. *Negotiation Journal, 5,* 265–278.

Rubin, J. Z., Pruitt, D. G., & Kim, S. H. (1994). *Social conflict: Escalation, stalemate, & settlement.* New York: McGraw-Hill.

Rubin, J. Z., & Rubin, C. (1989). *When families fight.* New York: William Morrow.

Rubinstein, R. A., & Foster, M. (Eds.). (1988). *The social dynamics of peace and conflict: Culture in international society.* Boulder, CO: Westview Press.

Schaap, C., Buunk, B., & Kerkstra, A. (1988). Marital conflict resolution. In P. Noller & M. A. Fitzpatrick (Eds.), *Perspectives on marital interaction* (pp. 203–244). Philadelphia: Multilingual Matters.

Schlueter, D. W., Barge, J. K., & Blankenship, D. (1990). A comparative analysis of influence strategies used by upper and lower-level male and female managers. *Western Journal of Speech Communication, 54*(1), 42–65.

Shailor, J. G. (1994). *Empowerment in dispute mediation: A critical analysis of communication.* Westport, CT: Praeger.

Shaw, M. (1994). Courts point justice in a new direction. *The National Law Journal, 4,* 11–94.

Sheppard, B. H. (1992). Conflict research as schizophrenia: The many faces of organizational conflict. *Journal of Organizational Behavior, 13,* 325–333.

Skratek, S. (1990). Grievance mediation: Does it really work? *Negotiation Journal, 6*(3), 269–280.

Stahler, G., DuCette, J., & Povich, E. (1990). Using mediation to prevent child maltreatment: An exploratory study. *Family Relations, 39,* 317–322.

Stamato, L. (1992). Sexual harassment in the workplace: Is mediation an appropriate forum? *Mediation Quarterly, 10*(2), 167–212.

Susskind, L., & Cruikshank, J. (1987). *Breaking the impasse: Consensual approaches to resolving public disputes.* New York: Basic Books.

Susskind, L., McKearnan, S., & Thomas-Larmer, J. (Eds.). (1999). *The consensus building handbook: A comprehensive guide to reaching agreement.* Thousand Oaks: Sage Publications.

Thomas, K. (1992). Conflict and conflict management: Reflections and update. *Journal of Organizational Behavior, 13,* 265–274.

Ting-Toomey, S. (1988). Intercultural conflict styles: A face-negotiation theory. In Y. Y. Kim & W. B. Gudykunst (Eds.), *Theories in intercultural communication* (pp. 213–238). Beverly Hills: Sage.

Ting-Toomey, S., Gao, G., Trubisky, P., Yang, Z., Kim, H. S., Ling, S-L., & Nishida, T. (1991). Culture, face maintenance, and styles of handling interpersonal conflict: A study of five cultures. *International Journal of Conflict Management, 2,* 275–296.

Tracy, K., & Spradlin, A. (1994). Talking like a mediator: Conversational moves of experienced divorce mediators. In J. P. Folger & T. S. Jones (Eds.), *New directions in mediation* (pp. 110–132). Thousand Oaks, CA: Sage.

Ury, W. L., Brett, J. M., & Goldberg, S. (1993). *Getting disputes resolved: Designing systems to cut the costs of conflict.* Cambridge, MA: Harvard Law School.

Vayrynen, R. (1991). To settle or to transform? Perspectives on the resolution of national and international conflicts. In R. Vayrynen (Ed.), *New directions in conflict theory* (pp. 1–25). Newbury Park, CA: Sage.

Vidmar, N. (1986). The mediation of small claims court disputes. In R. J. Lewicki, B. H. Sheppard, & M. H. Bazerman (Eds.), *Research on negotiation in organizations, Vol. 1* (pp. 187–208). Greenwich, CT: JAI Press.

Walker, G. B. (1990). Cultural orientations of argument in international disputes: Negotiating the law of the sea. In F. Korzenny & S. Ting-Toomey (Eds.), *Communicating for peace* (pp. 96–117). Newbury Park, CA: Sage.

Wall, J. A., Jr., & Rude, D. E. (1989). Judicial mediation of settlement negotiations. In K. Kressel & D. G. Pruitt (Eds.), *Mediation research: The process and effectiveness of third-party intervention* (pp. 190–212). San Francisco: Jossey-Bass.

Weber, A. L., Harvey, J. H., & Orbuch, T. L. (1992). What went wrong: Communicating accounts of relationship conflict. In M. L.

McLaughlin, M. J. Cody, & S. J. Read (Eds.), *Explaining one's self to others: Reason-giving in a social context* (pp. 261–280). Hillsdale, NJ: Lawrence Erlbaum.

Welton, G. L., Pruitt, D. G., & McGillicuddy, N. B. (1988). The role of caucusing in community mediation. *Journal of Conflict Resolution, 32*(1), 181–202.

Westin, A. F., & Feliu, A. G. (1988). *Resolving employment disputes without litigation.* Washington, DC: BNA Books.

Whelan, J. G. (1990). *The Moscow summit, 1988: Reagan and Gorbachev in negotiation.* Boulder, CO: Westview Press.

White, R. K. (1984). *Fearful warriors: A psychological profile of U.S.–Soviet relations.* New York: The Free Press.

Wilkins, A. L. (1989). *Developing corporate character: How to successfully change an organization without destroying it.* San Francisco: Jossey-Bass.

Wilkinson, J. H. (Ed.). (1990). *Donovan Leisure Newton and Irvine ADR practice book.* Colorado Springs: Wiley Law Publications.

Williams, G. (1983). *Legal negotiation and settlement.* St. Paul, MN: West.

Wilson, S. R., & Waltman, M. S. (1988). Assessing the Putnam–Wilson organizational communication conflict instrument (OCCI). *Management Communication Quarterly, 1,* 367–388.

Womack, D. F. (1988). A review of conflict instruments in organizational settings. *Management Communication Quarterly, 1,* 437–445.

Wondolleck, J. M. (1988). *Public lands conflict and resolution: Managing national forest disputes.* New York: Plenum Press.

Woodhouse, T. (1988). *The international peace directory.* Plymouth, UK: Northcote House Publishers.

Yale, D. (1988, Winter). Metaphors in mediating. *Mediation Quarterly, 22,* 15–24.

Young, O. (1972). Intermediaries: Additional thought on third parties. *Journal of Conflict Resolution, 16.*

Zartman, I. W., & Berman, M. (1982). *The practical negotiator.* New Haven, CT: Yale University Press.

Index